Emilia Pardo Bazan, Fanny Hale Gardiner

Russia

Its people and its literature

Emilia Pardo Bazan, Fanny Hale Gardiner

Russia

Its people and its literature

ISBN/EAN: 9783743333567

Manufactured in Europe, USA, Canada, Australia, Japa

Cover: Foto ©ninafisch / pixelio.de

Manufactured and distributed by brebook publishing software (www.brebook.com)

Emilia Pardo Bazan, Fanny Hale Gardiner

Russia

RUSSIA

ITS PEOPLE AND ITS LITERATURE

RUSSIA

ITS PEOPLE AND ITS LITERATURE

BY

EMILIA PARDO BAZÁN

Translated from the Spanish

By FANNY HALE GARDINER

CHICAGO
A. C. McCLURG & CO.
1901

COPYRIGHT,
BY A. C. MCCLURG AND CO.
A.D. 1890.

TRANSLATOR'S PREFACE.

EMILIA PARDO BAZÁN, the author of the following critical survey of Russian literature, is a Spanish woman of well-known literary attainments as well as wealth and position. Her life has been spent in association with men of mark, both during frequent sojourns at Madrid and at home in Galicia, "the Switzerland of Spain," from which province her father was a deputy to Cortes.

Books and libraries were almost her only pleasures in childhood, as she was allowed few companions, and she says she could never apply herself to music. By the time she was fourteen she had read widely in history, sciences, poetry, and fiction, excepting the works of the French romanticists, Dumas, George Sand, and Victor Hugo, which were forbidden fruit and were finally obtained and enjoyed as such. At sixteen she married and went to live in Madrid, where, amid the gayeties of the capital, her love for literature suffered a long eclipse.

Her father was obliged, for political reasons, to leave the country after the abdication of Amadeus, and she accompanied him in a long and to her profitable period of wandering, during which she learned French, English, and Italian, in order to read the literatures of those tongues. She also plunged deep into German philosophy, at first out of curiosity, because it was then in vogue; but she confesses a debt of gratitude to it nevertheless.

While she was thus absorbed in foreign tongues and literatures, she remained almost entirely ignorant of the new movement in her own land, led by Valera, Galdos, and Alarcon. The prostration which characterized the reign of Isabella II. had been followed by a rejuvenation born of the Revolution of 1868. When this new literature was at last brought to her notice, she read it with delighted surprise, and was immediately struck by something resembling the spirit of Cervantes, Hurtado, and other Spanish writers of old renown. Inspired by the possibility of this heredity, she resolved to try novel-writing herself, — a thought which had never occurred to her when her idea of the novel had been bounded by the romantic limitations of Victor Hugo and his suite. But if the novel might consist of descriptions of places and customs familiar to us, and studies of the people we see about us, then she would dare attempt it. As yet, however, no one talked of realism or naturalism in Spain; the tendency of Spanish writers was rather toward a restoration of elegant Castilian, and her own first novel followed this line, although evidently inspired by the breath of realism as far as she was then aware of it. The methods and objects of the French realists became fully manifest to her shortly afterward; for, being in poor health, she went to Vichy, where in hours of enforced leisure she read for the first time Balzac, Flaubert, Goncourt, and Daudet. The result led her to see the importance of their aims and the force of their art, to which she added the idea that each country should cultivate its own tradition while following the modern methods. These convictions she embodied first in a prologue to her second novel, "A Wedding Journey," and then in a series of articles published in the "Epoca" at Madrid, and afterward in Paris; these she avers were the first echoes in Spain of the French realist movement.

All of her novels have been influenced by the school of art to which she has devoted her attention and criticism, and her study of which has well qualified her for the essays contained in this volume. This work on Russian literature was published in 1887, but prior to its appearance in print the Señora de Bazán was invited to read selections from it before the Ateneo de Madrid, — an honor never before extended to a woman, I believe.

Few Spanish women are accustomed to speaking in public, and she thus describes her own first attempt in 1885, when, during the festivities attending the opening of the first railway between Madrid and Coruña, the capital of her native province, she was asked to address a large audience invited to honor the memory of a local poet : —

"Fearful of attempting so unusual a performance, as well as doubtful of the ability to make my voice heard in a large theatre, I took advantage of the presence of my friend Emilio Castelar to read to him my discourse and confide to him my fears. On the eve of the performance, Castelar, ensconced in an arm-chair in my library, puzzled his brains over the questions whether I should read standing or sitting, whether I should hold my papers in my hand or no, and having an artist's eye to the scenic effect, I think he would have liked to suggest that I pose before the mirror! But I was less troubled about my attitude than by the knowledge that Castelar was to speak also, and before me, which would hardly predispose my audience in my favor. . . . The theatre was crowded to suffocation, but I found that this rather animated than terrified me. I rose to read (for it was finally decided that I should stand), and I cannot tell how thin and hard and unsympathetic my voice sounded in the silence. My throat choked with emotion; but I was scarcely through the first paragraph when I heard at my right hand the voice of Castelar, low and earnest, saying over and over again, 'Very good, very good! That is the tone! So, so!' I breathed more freely, speaking became easier to me; and my audience, far from becoming impatient, gave me an attention and applause doubly grateful to one whose only hope had been to avoid a fiasco. Castelar greeted me at the close with a warm hand-grasp and beaming eyes, saying, 'We ought to be well satisfied, Emilia; we have achieved a notable and brilliant success; let us be happy, then!'"

Probably the Señora de Bazán learned her lesson well, and had no need of the friendly admonitions of Castelar when she came to address the distinguished audience at the Ateneo, for she is said to have "looked very much at ease," and to have been very well received, but a good deal criticised afterward, being the first Spanish woman who ever dared to read in the Ateneo.

Turning from the authoress to the work, I will only add that I hope the American reader may find it to be what it seemed to me as I read it in Spanish, — an epitome of a vast and elaborate subject, and a guide to a clear path through this maze which without a guide can hardly be clear to any but a profound student of belles-lettres; for classicism, romanticism, and realism are technical terms, and the purpose of the modern novel is only just beginning to be understood by even fairly intelligent readers. In the belief that the interest awakened by Russian literature is not ephemeral, and that this great, young, and original people has come upon the world's stage with a work to perform before the world's eye, I have translated this careful, critical, synthetical study of the Russian people and literature for the benefit of my intelligent countrymen.

F. H. G.

CHICAGO, March, 1890.

CONTENTS.

Book I.

THE EVOLUTION OF RUSSIA.

		PAGE
I.	Scope and Purpose of the Present Essay	11
II.	The Russian Country	17
III.	The Russian Race	26
IV.	Russian History	41
V.	The Russian Autocracy	49
VI.	The Agrarian Communes	64
VII.	Social Classes in Russia	83
VIII.	Russian Serfdom	95

Book II.

RUSSIAN NIHILISM AND ITS LITERATURE.

I.	The Word "Nihilism"	107
II.	Origin of the Intellectual Revolution	113
III.	Woman and the Family	117
IV.	Going to the People	125
V.	Herzen and the Nihilist Novel	132
VI.	The Reign of Terror	140
VII.	The Police and the Censor	147

Book III.

RISE OF THE RUSSIAN NOVEL.

		PAGE
I.	The Beginnings of Russian Literature	155
II.	Russian Romanticism.— The Lyric Poets	165
III.	Russian Realism: Gogol, its Founder	178

Book IV.

MODERN RUSSIAN REALISM.

I.	Turguenief, Poet and Artist	209
II.	Gontcharof and Oblomovism	233
III.	Dostoiëwsky, Psychologist and Visionary	236
IV.	Tolstoï, Nihilist and Mystic	255
V.	French Realism and Russian Realism	274

Book I.

THE EVOLUTION OF RUSSIA.

I.

SCOPE AND PURPOSE OF THE PRESENT ESSAY.

THE idea of writing something about Russia, the Russian novel, and Russian social conditions (all of which bear an intimate relationship to one another), occurred to me during a sojourn in Paris, where I was struck with the popularity and success achieved by the Russian authors, and especially the novelists. I remember that it was in the month of March, 1885, that the Russian novel "Crime and Punishment," by Dostoïewsky, fell into my hands and left on my mind a deep impression. Circumstances prevented my following up at that time my idea of literary work on the subject; but the next winter I had nothing more important to do than to make my projected excursion into this new realm.

My interest was quickened by all the reports I read of those who had done the same. They all declared that one branch of Russian literature, that which flourishes to-day in every part of Europe, namely, the novel, has no rival in any other nation, and that the so much discussed tendency to the preeminence of truth in art, variously called realism, naturalism, etc., has existed in the Russian novel ever since the Romantic period, a full quarter of a century earlier than in France. I saw also that the more refined and select portion of the Parisian public, that part which boasts an educated and exacting taste, bought and devoured the works of Turguénief, Tolstoï, and Dostoïewsky with as much eagerness as those of Zola, Goncourt, and Daudet; and it was useless to ascribe this universal eagerness merely to a conspiracy intended to produce jealousy and humiliation among the masters and leaders of naturalism or realism in France, even though I may be aware that such a conspiracy tacitly exists, as well as a certain amount of involuntary jealousy, which, in fact, even the most illustrious artist is prone to display.

I do not ignore the objections that might be urged against going to foreign lands in search of novelties, and I should decline to face them if Russian literature were but one of the many caprices of the exhausted Parisian imagination. I know very well that the French capital is a city of novelties, hungry for extravagances which may entertain for a moment and appease its yawning weariness, and that to this necessity for diversion the *decadent* school (which has lately had such a revival, and claims the aberrations of the Spanish Gongora as its master), though aided by some talent and some technical skill, owes the favor it enjoys. Some years ago I attended a concert in Paris, where I heard an orchestra of Bohemians, or Zingaras, itinerant musicians from Hungary. I was asked my opinion of them at the close, and I frankly confessed that the orchestra sounded to me very like a jangling of mule-bells or a caterwauling; they were only a little more tolerable than a street band of my own country (Spain), and only because these were gypsies were their scrapings to be endured at all. Literary oddities are puffed and made much of by certain Parisian critics very much as the Bohemian musicians were, as, for example, the Japanese novel "The Loyal Ronins," and certain romantic sketches of North American origin.

It is but just, nevertheless, to acknowledge that in France the mania for the exotic has a laudable aim and obeys an instinct of equity. To know everything, to call nothing outlandish, to accord the highest right of human citizenship, the right of creating their own art and of sacrificing according to their own rites and customs on the altar sacred to Beauty, not only to the great nations, but to the decayed and obscure ones, — this surely is a generous act on the part of a people endowed with directive energies; the more so as, in order to do this, the French have to overcome a certain petulant vanity which naturally leads them to consider themselves not merely the first but the only people.

But confining myself now to Russia, I do not deny that to my curiosity there were added certain doubts as to the value of her literary treasures. During my investigations, however, I have discovered that, apart from the intrinsic merit of her famous authors, her literature must attract our attention because of its intimate connections with social, political, and historical problems which are occupying the mind of Europe to-day, and are outcomes of the great revolutionary movement, unless it would be more correct to say that they inspired and directed that movement.

I take this opportunity to confess frankly that I lack one almost indispensable qualification for my task, — the knowledge of the Russian language. It would have been easy for me, during my residence in Paris, to acquire a smattering of it perhaps, enough to conceal my ignorance and to enable me to read some selections in poetry and prose; but not so easy thus to learn thoroughly a language which for intricacy, splendid coloring, and marvellous flexibility and harmony can only be compared, in the opinion of philologists, to the ancient Greek. Of what use then a mere smattering, which would be insufficient to give to my studies a positive character and an indisputable authority? Two years would not have been too long to devote to such an accomplishment, and in that length of time new ideas, different lines of thought, and unexpected obstacles might perhaps arise; the opportunity would be gone and my plan would have lost interest.

Still, I mentioned my scruples on this head to certain competent persons, and they agreed that ignorance of the Russian language, though an ignorance scarcely uncommon, would be an insuperable difficulty if I proposed to write a didactic treatise upon

Russian letters, instead of a rapid review or a mere sketch in the form of a modest essay or two. They added that the best Russian books were translated into French or German, and that in these languages, and also in English and Italian, had been published several able and clever works relative to Muscovite literature and institutions, solid enough foundations upon which to build my efforts.

It may be said, and with good reason, that if I could not learn the language I might at least have made a trip to Russia, and like Madame de Staël when she revealed to her countrymen the culture of a foreign land, see the places and people with my own eyes. But Russia is not just around the corner, and the women of my country, though not cowardly, are not accustomed to travel so intrepidly as for example the women of Great Britain. I have often envied the good fortune of that clever Scotchman, Mackenzie Wallace, who has explored the whole empire of Russia, ridden in sleighs over her frozen rivers, chatted with peasants and *popes*, slept beneath the tents of the nomadic tribes, and shared their offered refreshment of fermented mare's-milk, the only delicacy their patriarchal hospitality afforded. But I acknowledge my deficiencies, and can only hope that some one better qualified than I may take up and carry on this imperfect and tentative attempt.

I have tried to supply from other sources those things which I lacked. Not only have I read everything written upon Russia in every language with which I am acquainted, but I have associated myself with Russian writers and artists, and noted the opinions of well-informed persons (who often, however, be it said in parenthesis, only served to confuse me by their differences and opposition). A good part of the books (a list of which I give at the end) were hardly of use to me, and I read them merely from motives of literary honesty. To save continual references I prefer to speak at once and now of those which I used principally: Mackenzie Wallace's work entitled "Russia" abounds in practical insight and appreciation; Anatole Leroy-Beaulieu's "The Empire of the Czars" is a profound, exact, and finished study, so acknowledged even by the Russians themselves in their most just and calm judgments; Tikomirov's "Russia, Political and Social" is clear and comprehensible, though rather radical and passionate, as might be expected of the work of an exile; Melchior de Voguié's "The Russian Novel" is a critical study of incomparable delicacy, though I do not always acquiesce in his conclusions. From these four books, to which I would add the remarkable "History of Russia" by Rambaud, I have drawn copious draughts; and giving them this mention, I may dispense with further reference to them.

II.

THE RUSSIAN COUNTRY.

If we consider the present state of European nations, we shall observe a decided decline of the political fever which excited them from about the end of the last century to the middle of the present one. A certain calm, almost a stagnation with some, has followed upon the conquest of rights more craved than appreciated. The idea of socialistic reforms is agitated darkly and threateningly among the masses, openly declaring itself from time to time in strikes and riots; but on the other hand, the middle classes almost everywhere are anxious for a long respite in which to enjoy the new social conditions created by themselves and for themselves. The middle classes represent the largest amount of intellectual force; they have withdrawn voluntarily (through egoism, prudence, or indifference) from active political fields, and renounced further efforts in the line of experiment; the arts and letters, which are in the main the work of well-to-do people, cry out against this withdrawal, and, losing all social affinities, become likewise isolated.

France possesses at this moment that form of government for which she yearned so long and so convulsively; yet she has not found in it the sort of well-being she most desired, — that industrial and economical prosperity, that coveted satisfaction and compensation which should restore to the Cock of Brenus his glittering spurs and scarlet crest. She is at peace, but doubtful of herself, always fearful of having to behold again the vandalism of the Commune and the catastrophes of the Prussian invasion. Italy, united and restored, has not regained her place as a European power, nor, in rising again from her glorious ashes, can she reanimate the dust of the heroes, the great captains and the sublime artists, that lie beneath her monuments. And it is not only the Latin nations that stand in more or less anxious expectation of the future. If France has established her much desired republic, and Italy has accomplished her union, England also has tasted all the fruits of the parliamentary system, has imparted her vigor to magnificent colonies, has succeeded in impressing her political doctrines and her positive ideas of life upon the whole continent; while Germany has obtained the military supremacy and the amalgamation of the fatherland once dismembered by feudalism, as well as the fulfilment of the old Teutonic dream of Cæsarian power and an imperial throne, — a dream cherished since the Middle Ages. For the Saxon races the hour of change has sounded too; in a certain way they have fulfilled their destinies, they have accomplished their historic work, and I think I see them like actors on the stage declaiming the closing words of their rôles.

One plain symptom of what I have described seems to me to be the draining off of their creative forces in the domain of art. What proportion does the artistic energy of England and Germany bear to their political strength? None at all. No names nowadays cross the Channel to be put up beside — I will not say those of Shakspeare and Byron, but even those of Walter Scott and Dickens; there is no one to wear the mantle of the illustrious author of "Adam Bede," who was the incarnation of the moral sense and temperate realism of her country, and at the same time an eloquent witness to the extent and limit allowed by these two tendencies, both of puritanic origin, to the laws of æsthetics and poetry. On the other side of the Rhine the tree of Romance is dry, though its roots are buried in the mysterious subsoil of legend, and beneath its branches pass and repass the heroes of the ballads of Bürger and Goethe, and within its foliage are crystallized the brilliant dialectics of Hegel. To put it plainly, Germany to-day produces nothing within herself, particularly if we compare this to-day with the not distant yesterday.

But I would be less general, and set forth my idea in a clearer manner. It is not my purpose to sacrifice on the altar of my theme the genius of all Europe. I recognize willingly that there are in every nation writers worthy of distinction and praise, and not only in nations of the first rank but in some also of second and third, as witness those of Portugal, Belgium, Sweden, modern Greece, Denmark, and even Roumania, which can boast a queenly authoress, extremely talented and sympathetic. I merely say — and to the intelligent reader I need give but few reasons why — that it is easy to distinguish the period in which a people, without being actually sterile, and even displaying relatively a certain fecundity which may deceive the superficial observer, yet ceases to produce anything virile and genuine, or to possess vital and creative powers.

To this general rule I consider France an exception, for she is really the only nation which, since the close of the Romantic period, has seen any spontaneous literary production great enough to traverse and influence all Europe, — a phenomenon which cannot be explained by the mere fact of the general use of the French tongue and customs. It will be understood that I refer to the rise and success of Realism, and that I speak of it in a large sense, not limiting my thoughts to the master minds, but considering it in its entirety, from its origin to its newest ramifications, from its antecedent encyclopedists to its latest echoes, the pessimists, *decadents*, and other fanatics. Looking at what are called French naturalists or realists in a group, as a unity which obliterates details, I cannot deny to France the glory of presenting to the world in the second half of this century a literary development, which, even if it carries within itself the germs of senility and decrepitude (namely, the very materialism which is its philosophic basis, its very extremes and exaggerations, and its erudite and reflective character, a quality which however unapparent is nevertheless perfectly demonstrable), yet it shows also the vigor of a renaissance in its valiant affirmation of artistic truth, its zeal in maintaining this, in the faith with which it seeks this truth, and in the effectiveness of its occasional revelations thereof. When party feeling has somewhat subsided, French realism will receive due thanks for the impulse it has communicated to other peoples; not a lamentable impulse either, for nations endowed with robust national traditions always know how to give form and shape to whatever comes to them from without, and those only will accept a completed art who lack the true conditions of nationality, even though they figure as States on the map.

There are two great peoples in the world which are not in the same situation as the Latin and Saxon nations of Europe, — two peoples which have not yet placed their stones in the world's historic edifice. They are the great transatlantic republic and the colossal Sclavonic empire, — the United States and Russia.

What artistic future awaits the young North American nation? That land of material civilization, free, happy, with wise and practical institutions, with splendid natural resources, with flourishing commerce and industries, that people so young yet so vigorous, has acquired everything except the acclimatization in her vast and fertile territory of the flower of beauty in the arts and letters. Her literature, in which such names as Edgar Poe shine with a world-wide lustre, is yet a prolongation of the English literature, and no more. What would that country not give to see within herself the glorious promise of that spirit which produced a Murillo, a Cervantes, a Goethe, or a Meyerbeer, while she covers with gold the canvases of the mediocre painters of Europe!

But that art and literature of a national character may be spontaneous, a people must pass through two epochs, — one in which, by the process of time, the myths and heroes of earlier days assume a representative character, and the early creeds and aspirations, still undefined by reflection, take shape in popular poetry and legend; the other in which, after a period of learning, the people arises and shakes off the outer crust of artificiality, and begins to build conscientiously its own art upon the basis of its never-forgotten traditions. The United States was born full-grown. It never passed through the cloudland of myth; it is utterly lacking in that sort of popular poetry which to-day we call folk-lore.

But when a nation carries within itself this powerful and prolific seed, sooner or later this will sprout. A people may be silent for long years, for ages, but at the first rays of its dawning future it will sing like the sphinx of Egypt. Russia is a complete proof of this truth. Perhaps no other nation ever saw its æsthetic development unfold so unpromisingly, so cramped and so stunted. The stiff and unyielding garments of French classicism have compressed the spirit of its national literature almost to suffocation; German Romanticism, since the beginning of this century, has lorded it triumphantly there more than in any other land. But in spite of so many obstacles, the genius of Russia has made a way for itself, and to-day offers us a sight which other nations can only parallel in their past history; namely, the sudden revelation of a national literature.

I do not mean to prophesy for others an irremediable sterility or decadence; I merely confine myself to noting one fact: Russia is at this moment the only young nation in Europe,—the last to arrive at the banquet. The rest live upon their past; this one sets out now impetuously to conquer the future. Over Russia are passing at present the hours of dawn, the golden days, the times that after a while will be called classic; some even of the men whom generations to come will call their glorious ancestors are living now. I insist upon this view in order to explain the curiosity which this empire of the North has aroused in Europe, and also to explain why so much thoughtful and serious study and attention is given to Russia by all foreigners; while every book or article on such a country as Spain, for instance, is full of so many careless and superficial errors. That elegant and subtle author, Voguié, in writing of Léon Tolstoï, says that this Russian novelist is so great that he seems to belong to the dead,— meaning to express in this wise the idea that the magnitude of Tolstoï's genius annuls the laws of temporal criticism by which we are accustomed to see the glory of our contemporaries less or more than the reality. I would apply Voguié's phrase to the Russian national literature as a whole. Though I see it arise before my very eyes, yet I view it amid the halo of prestige enjoyed only by things that have been.

There is indeed no parallel to it anywhere. The modern phenomenon of the resurrection of local literatures, and the reappearance of forgotten or amalgamated races, bears no analogy to this Russian movement; for apart from the fact that the former represents a protest by race individualism against dominant nationalities, and the latter, on the contrary, bears the seal of strong unity of sentiment (which distinguishes Russia), it must be borne in mind that local literatures are reactionary in themselves, — restorers of traditions more or less forgotten and lost sight of, — while Russian literature is an innovation, which accepts the past, not as its ideal, but as its root.

I have heard Émile Zola say, with his usual ingenuousness, that between his own spirit and that of the Russian novel there was something like a haze. This gray vapor may be the effect of the northern mist which is so asphyxiating to Latin brains, or it may be owing to the eccentricity which sometimes produces a work entirely independent of accepted social notions and historical factors. In order to dissipate this haze, this mist, I must devote a part of this essay to a study of the race, the natural conditions, the history, the institutions, the social and political state of Russia, especially to that revolutionary effervescence known as Nihilism. Without such a preliminary study I could scarcely give any idea of this literary phenomenon.

Let us, then, cross the Russian frontier and enter her colossal expanse, without being too much abashed by its size, which, says Humboldt, is greater than that of the disk of the full moon. Really, when we cast our eyes upon the map, fancy refuses to believe or to conceive that so large an extent of territory can form but one nation and obey but one man. We are amazed by its geographical bigness, and a sentiment of respect involuntarily enters the mind, together with the instinctive conviction that God has not modelled the body of this Titan without having in view for it some admirable historical destiny to be achieved by the fine diplomacy of Providence. Truly it is God's handiwork, as is proved by its solid unity, — geographical as well as ethnographical, — and its duration as an independent empire. Russia is no artificial conglomeration, nor a federation of States, — each with distinct internal life and traditions, — the result of conquest or of the necessity of resistance to a common enemy; for while the strife against the nomadic Asiatics may have contributed to solidify her union, it was Nature that predisposed her to a community of aspirations and political existence. There are islands like Sicily, peninsulas like Spain, whose territory, though so small, is far more easily subdivided than Russia, which is intersected by no mountain chains, and which is everywhere connected by rivers, — water-ways of communication. The vast surface of Russia is like a piece of cloth which unfolds everywhere alike, seamless and level. The northern regions, which produce lumber, cannot exist without the southern regions, which produce cereals; the two halves of Russia are complementary; there is nowhere any conception of the provincialisms which honeycomb the Spanish peninsula; and in spite of the imposing magnitude of the nation, which at first glance would seem necessarily divided into different if not inimical provinces, especially those most distant, the cohesion is so strong that all Russia considers herself, not so much a state as a family, subject to the law of a father; and Father they call, with tender familiarity, the Autocrat of all the Russias. Even to-day the name of the famous Mazeppa, who tried to separate Ukrania from Russia, is a term of insult in the Ukranian dialect, and his name is cursed in their temples. To this sublime sentiment Russia owes that national independence which the other Sclavonic peoples have lost.

III.

THE RUSSIAN RACE.

It is no hindrance to Muscovite unity that within it there are two completely opposing elements, namely, the Germanic and the Semitic. The influence of the Germans is about as irritating to the Russians as was that of the Flemings to the Spaniards under Charles V. They are petted and protected by the government, especially in the Baltic provinces, all the while that the Russians accuse them of having introduced two abominations, — bureaucracy and despotism. But even more aggravating to the Russian is the Jewish usurer, who since the Middle Ages has fastened himself like a leach upon producer and consumer, and who, if he does not borrow or lend, begs; and if he does not beg, carries on some suspicious business. A nation within a nation, the Jews are sometimes made the victims of popular hatred; the usually gentle Russians sometimes rise in sudden wrath, and the newspapers report to us dreadful accounts of an assault and murder of Hebrews.

Russian national unity is not founded, however, upon community of race; on the contrary, nowhere on the globe are the races and tribes more numerous than those that have spread over that illimitable territory like the waves of the sea; and as the high tide washes away the marks of every previous wave, and levels the sandy surface, these divers races have gone on stratifying, each forgetful of its distinct origin. Those who study Russian ethnography call it a chaos, and declare that at least twenty layers of human alluvium exist in European Russia alone, without counting the emigrations of prehistoric peoples whose names are lost in oblivion. And yet from these varied races and origins — Scythians, Sarmatians, Kelts, Germans, Goths, Tartars, and Mongols — has proceeded a most homogeneous people, a most solid coalescence, little given to treasuring up ancient rights and lost causes. Geographical oneness has superseded ethnographical variety, and created a moral unity stronger than all other.

When so many races spread themselves over one country, it becomes necessary and inevitable that one shall exercise sovereignty. In Russia this directive and dominant race was the Sclav, not because of numerical superiority, but from a higher character more adaptable to European civilization, and perhaps by virtue of its capability for expansion. Compare the ethnographical maps of Russia in the ninth and nineteenth centuries. In the ninth the Sclavs occupy a spot which is scarcely a fifth part of European Russia; in the nineteenth the spot has spread like oil, covering two thirds of the Russian map. And as the Sclavonic inundation advances, the inferior races recede toward the frozen pole or the deserts of Asia. When the monk Nestor wrote the first account of Russia, the Sclavs lived hedged in by Lithuanians, Turks, and Finns; to-day they number above sixty million souls.

Thus it is once more demonstrated that to the Aryan race, naturally and without violence, is reserved the pre-eminence in modern civilization. A thousand years ago northern Russia was peopled by Finnish tribes; in still more recent times the Asiatic fisherman cast his nets where now stands the capital of Peter the Great; and yet without any war of extermination, without any emigration of masses, without persecutions, or the deprivation of legal privileges, the aboriginal Finns have subsided, have been absorbed, — have become Russianized, in a word.

This is not surprising, perhaps, to us who believe in the absolute superiority of the Indo-European race, noble, high-minded, capable of the loftiest and profoundest conceptions possible to the human intellect. I may say that the Russian ethnographical evolution may be compared with that of my own country, if we may trust recent and well-authenticated theories. The most remote peoples of Russia were, like those of Spain, of Turanian origin, with flattish faces, and high cheek-bones, speaking a soft-flowing language; and to this day, as in Spain also, one may see in some of the physiognomies clear traces of the old blood in spite of the predominance of the invading Aryan. In Spain, perhaps, the aboriginal Turanian bequeathed no proofs of intellectual keenness to posterity, and the famous Basque songs and legends of Lelo and Altobizkar may turn out to be merely clever modern tricks of imitation; but in Russia the Finnish element, whose influence is yet felt, shows great creative powers. One of the richest popular literatures known to the researches of folklore is the epic cycle of Finland called the Kalevala, which compares with the Sanscrit poems of old.

A Castilian writer of note, absent at present from his country, in writing to me privately his opinions on Russia, said that the civilization which we behold has been created, so far as concerns its good points, exclusively by the Mediterranean race dwelling around that sea of inspiration which stretches from the Pillars of Hercules to Tyre and Sidon; that sea which brought forth prophets, incarnate gods, great captains and navigators, arch-philosophers, and the geniuses of mankind. Recently the most celebrated of our orators has stirred up in Paris some Greco-Latin manifestations whose political opportuneness is not to the point just here, but whose ethnographical significance, seeking to divide Europe into northern barbarians and civilized Latin folk, — just as happened at the fall of the Roman Empire, — is of no benefit to me. Who would listen without protest nowadays to the famous saying that the North has given us only iron and barbarism, or read tranquilly Grenville Murray's exclamation in an access of Britannic patriotism, "Russia will fall into a thousand pieces, the common fate of barbarous States!" The intelligence of the hearers would be offended, for they would recall the part played in universal civilization by Germans and Saxons, — Germany, Holland, England; but confining myself to the subject in hand, I cannot credit those who taunt the Sclav with being a barbarian, when he is as much an Aryan, a descendant of Japhet, as the Latin, descended as much as he from the sacred sources beside which lay the cradle of humanity, and where it first received the revelation of the light. Knowing their origin, are we to judge the Sclav as the Greeks, the contemporaries of Herodotus, did the Scythian and the Sarmatian, relegating him forever to the cold eternal night of Cimmerian regions?

It is nothing remarkable that, in the varied fortunes of this great Indo-European family of races, if the Kelt came early to the front, the Sclav came correspondingly late. Who can explain the causes of this diversity of destiny between the two branches that most resemble each other on this great tree?

In the study of Russian writings I was ofttimes surprised at the resemblances in the character, customs, and modes of thought of the Russian *mujik* to those of the peasants of Gallicia (northern Spain), my native province. Then I read in various authors that the Sclav is more like the Kelt than like his other ancestors, which observation applied equally well to my own people. Perhaps the Kelt brought to Spain and France the first seeds of civilization; but the superiority of the Greek and the Latin obliterated the traces of that primitive culture which has left us no written monuments. More fortunate is the Sclav, the last to put his hand to the great work, for he is sure of leaving the marks of his footprints upon the sands of time.

It is undeniable that he has come late upon the world's stage, and after the ages of inspiration and of brilliant historic action have passed. It sometimes seems now as though the brain of the world had lost its freshness and plastic quality, as though every possible phase of civilization had been seen in Greece and Rome, the Middle Ages and the Renaissance, and in the scientific and political development of our own day. But the backwardness of the Russian has been caused by no congenital inferiority of race; his quickness and aptitude are apparent, and sufficient to prove it is the rich treasure of popular poetry to be found among the peoples of Sclav blood, — Servians, Russians, and Poles. Such testimony is irrefutable, and is to groups of peoples what articulate speech is to the individual in the zoölogical scale. What the Romanceros are to the Spaniard, the Bilinas are to the Russian, — an immense collection of songs in which the people have immortalized the memory of persons and events indelibly engraved on their imagination; a copious spring, a living fountain, whither the future bards of Russia must return to drink of originality. What the poem of the Cid represents to Spain, and the Song of Roland to France, is symbolized for the Russian by the Song of the Tribe of Igor, the work of some anonymous Homer, — a pantheistic epic impregnated with the abounding and almost overwhelming sense of realism which seems to preponderate in the literary genius of Russia.

History — and I use this word in the broadest sense known to us to-day — thrusts some nations to the fore, as the Latins, for example; others, like the Sclavs, she holds back, restraining their instinctive efforts to make themselves heard. We are accustomed to say that Russia is an Asiatic country, and that the Russian is a Tartar with a thin coat of European polish. The Mongolian element must certainly be taken into account in a study of Muscovite ethnography, in spite of the supremacy of the Byzantine and Tartar influence, and in order to understand Russia. In the interior of European Russia the ugly *Kalmuk* is still to be seen, and who can say how many drops of Asiatic blood run in the veins of some of the most illustrious Russian families? Yet within this question of purity of race lies a scientific and social *quid* easily demonstrable according to recent startling biological theories, and only the thoughtless will censure the old Spaniards for their efforts to prove their blood free of any taint of Moor or Jew. Russia, with her double nature of European and Asiatic, seems like a princess in a fairy-tale turned to stone by a malignant sorcerer's art, but restored to her natural and living form by the magic word of some valiant knight. Her face, her hands, and her beautiful figure are already warm and lifelike, but her feet are still immovable as stone, though the damsel struggles for the fulness of reanimation; even so Imperial Russia strives to become entirely European, to free herself from Asiatic inertia to-day.

Apart from the undeniable Asiatic influence, we must consider the extreme and cruel climate as among the causes of her backwardness. The young civilization flourishes under soft skies, beside blue seas whose soft waves lave the limbs of the new-born goddess. Where Nature ill-treats man he needs twice the time and labor to develop his vocation and tendencies. To us of a more temperate zone, the description of the rigorous and overpowering climate of Russia is as full of terrors as Dante's Inferno. The formation of the land only adds to the trying conditions of the atmosphere. Russia consists of a series of plains and table-lands without mountains, without seas or lakes worthy of the name, — for those that wash her coasts are considered scarcely navigable. The only fragments of a mountain system are known by the generic and expressive term *ural*, meaning a girdle; and in truth they serve only to engirdle the whole territory. To an inhabitant of the interior the sight of a mountainous country is entirely novel and surprising. Almost all the Russian poets and novelists exiled to the Caucasus have found an unexpected fountain of inspiration in the panorama which the mountains afforded to their view. The hero of Tolstoï's novel "The Cossacks," on arriving at the Caucasus for the first time, and finding himself face to face with a mountain, stands mute and amazed at its sublime beauty.

"What is that?" he asked the driver of his cart.

"The mountain," is the indifferent reply.

"What a beautiful thing!" exclaims the traveller, filled with enthusiasm. "Nobody at home can imagine anything like it!" And he loses himself in the contemplation of the snow-covered crests rising abruptly above the surface of the steppes.

The oceans that lie upon the boundaries of Russia send no refreshing breezes over her vast continental expanse, for the White Sea, the Arctic, the Baltic, and sometimes the Caspian, are often ice-bound, while the waves of the Sea of Asof are turbid with the slime of marshes. Neither does Russia enjoy the mild influence of the Gulf Stream, whose last beneficent waves subside on the shores of Scandinavia. The winds from the Arctic region sweep over the whole surface unhindered all the winter long, while in the short summer the fiery breath of the central Asian deserts, rolling over the treeless steppes, bring an intolerable heat and a desolating drought. Beyond Astrakan the mercury freezes in winter and bursts in the summer sun. Under the rigid folds of her winter shroud Russia sleeps the sleep of death long months at a time, and upon her lifeless body slowly and pauselessly fall the "white feathers" of which Herodotus speaks; the earth becomes marble, the air a knife. A snow-covered country is a beautiful sight when viewed through a stereopticon, or from the comfortable depths of a fur-lined, swift-gliding sleigh; but snow is a terrible adversary to human activity. If its effects are not as dissipating as excessive heat, it none the less pinches the soul and paralyzes the body. In extreme climates man has a hard time of it, and Nature proves the saying of Goethe: "It envelops and governs us; we are incapable of combating it, and likewise incapable of eluding its tyrannical power." Formidable in its winter sleep, Nature appears even more despotic perhaps in its violent resurrection, when it breaks its icy bars and passes at once from lethargy to an almost fierce and frenzied life. In the spring-time Russia is an eruption, a surprise; the days lengthen with magic rapidity; the plants leaf out, and the fruits ripen as though by enchantment; night comes hardly at all, but instead a dusky twilight falls over the land; vegetation runs wild, as though with impatience, knowing that its season of happiness will be short. The great writer, Nicolaï Gogol, depicts the spring-time on the Russian steppes in the following words:

"No plough ever furrowed the boundless undulations of this wild vegetation. Only the unbridled herds have ever opened a path through this impenetrable wilderness. The face of earth is like a sea of golden verdure, broken into a thousand shades. Among the thin, dry branches of the taller shrubs climb the cornflowers, — blue, purple, and red; the broom lifts its pyramid of yellow flowers; tufts of white clover dot the dark earth, and beneath their poor shade glides the agile partridge with outstretched neck. The chattering of birds fills the air; the sparrow-hawk hangs motionless overhead, or beats the air with the tips of his wings, or swoops upon his prey with searching eyes. At a distance one hears the sharp cry of a flock of wild duck, hovering like a dark cloud over some lake lost or unseen in the immensity of the plain. The prairie-gull rises with a rhythmic movement, bathing his shining plumage in the blue air; now he is a mere speck in the distance, once more he glistens white and brilliant in the rays of the sun, and then disappears. When evening begins to fall, the steppes become quite still; their whole breadth burns under the last ardent beams; it darkens quickly, and the long shadows cover the ground like a dark pall of dull and equal green. Then the vapors thicken;.each flower, each herb, exhales its aroma, and all the plain is steeped in perfume. The crickets chirp vigorously. . . . . At night the stars look down upon the sleeping Cossack, who, if he opens his eyes, will see the steppes illuminated with sparks of light, — the fireflies. Sometimes the dark depths of the sky are lighted up by fires among the dry reeds that line the banks of the little streams and lakes, and long lines of swans, flying northward and disclosed to view by this weird light, seem like bands of red crossing the sky."

Do we not seem to see in this description the growth of this impetuous, ardent, spasmodic life, goaded on to quick maturity by the knowledge of its own brevity?

Without entirely accepting Montesquieu's theory as to climate, it is safe to allow that it contains a large share of truth. It is indubitable that the influence of climate is to put conditions to man's artistic development by forcing him to keep his gaze fixed upon the phenomena of Nature and the alternation and contrast of seasons, and helps to develop in him a fine pictorial sense of landscape, as in the case of the Russian writers. In our temperate zone we may live in relative independence of the outside world, and almost insensible to the transition from summer to winter. We do not have to battle with the atmosphere; we breathe it, we float in it. Perhaps for this reason good word-painters of landscape are few in our (Spanish) literature, and our descriptive poets content themselves with stale and regular phrases about the aurora and the sunset. But laying aside this parallel, which perhaps errs in being over-subtle, I will say that I agree with those who ascribe to the Russian climate a marked influence in the evolution of Russian character, institutions, and history.

Enveloped in snow and beaten by the north wind, the Sclav wages an interminable battle; he builds him a light sleigh by whose aid he subjects the frozen rivers to his service; he strips the animals of their soft skins for his own covering; to accustom his body to the violent transitions and changes of temperature, he steams himself in hot vapors, showers himself with cold water, and then lashes himself with a whip of cords, and if he feels a treacherous languor in his blood he rubs and rolls his body in the snow, seeking health and stimulus from his very enemy. But strong as is his power of reaction and moral energy, put this man, overwrought and wearied, beside a genial fire, in the silence of the tightly closed *isba*, or hut, within his reach a jug of *kvass* or *wodka* (a terrible *fire-water* more burning than any other), and, obeying the urgency of the long and cruel cold, he drinks himself into a drunken sleep, his senses become blunted, and his brain is overcome with drowsiness. Do not exact of him the persevering activity of the German, nor talk to him of the public life which is adapted to the Latin mind. Who can imagine a forum, an oracle, a tribune, in Russia? Study the effect of an inclement sky upon a Southern mind in the Elegies of Ovid banished to the Pontus; his reiterated laments inspire a profound pity, like the piping of a sick bird cowering in the harsh wind. The poet's greatest dread is that his bones may lie under the earth of Sarmatia; he, the Latin voluptuary, son of a race that desires for its dead that the earth may lie lightly on them, shrinks in anticipation of the cold beyond the tomb, when he thinks that his remains may one day be covered by that icy soil.

The Sclav is the victim of his climate, which relaxes his fibres and clouds his spirit. The Sclav, say those who know him well, lacks tenacity, firmness; he is flexible and variable in his impressions; as easily enthusiastic as indifferent; fluctuating between opposite conclusions; quick to assimilate foreign ideas; as quick to rid himself of them; inclined to dreamy indolence and silent reveries; given to extremes of exaltation and abasement; in fact, much resembling the climate to which he has to adapt himself. It needs not be said that this description, and any other which pretends to sum up the characteristics of the whole people, must have numerous exceptions, not only in individual cases but in whole groups within the Russian nationality: the Southerner will be more lively and vivacious; the Muscovite (those properly answering to that name) more dignified and stable; the Finlander, serious and industrious, like the Swiss, to whose position his own is somewhat analogous. There is in every nation a psychical as well as physical type to which the rank and file more or less correspond, and it is only upon a close scrutiny that one notices differences. The influence of the Tropics upon the human race has never been denied; we are forced to admit the influence of the Pole also, which, while beneficial in those lands not too close upon it, invigorating both bodies and souls and producing those chaste and robust barbarians who were the regenerators of the effete Empire, yet too close, it destroys, it annihilates. Who can doubt the effect of the snow upon the Russian character when it is stated upon the authority of positive data and statistics that the vice of drunkenness increases in direct proportion to the degrees of latitude? There is a fine Russian novel, "Oblomoff" (of which I shall speak again later), which is more instructive than a long dissertation. The apathy, the distinctively Russian enervation of the hero, puts the languor of the most indolent Creole quite in the shade, with the difference that in the case of the Sclav brain and imagination are at work, and his body, if well wrapped, is able to enjoy the air of a not unendurable temperature.

Not only the rigors of climate but the aspect of the outside world has a marked influence on character. Ovid in exile lamented having to live where the fields produced neither fruits nor sweet grapes; he might have added, had he lived in Russia, where the fields are all alike, where the eye encounters no variety to attract and please it. Castile is flat and monotonous like Russia, but there the sky compensates for the nakedness of the earth, and one cannot be sad beneath that canopy of turquoise blue. In Russia the dark firmament seems a leaden vault instead of a silken canopy, and oppresses the breast. The only things to diversify the immense expanse of earth are the great rivers and the broad belts or zones of the land, which may be divided into the northern, covered with forests; the *black lands*, which have been the granary of the empire from time immemorial; the arable steppes, so beautifully described by Gogol, like the American prairies, the land of the wild horses of the Russian heroic age; and lastly, the sandy steppes, sterile deserts only inhabited by the nomadic shepherds and their flocks. Throughout this vast body four large arteries convey the lifegiving waters: the Dnieper which brought to Russia the culture of old Byzantium; the Neva, beside which sits the capital of its modern civilization; the Don, legendary and romantic; and the Volga, the great *Mother Volga*, the marvellous river, whose waters produce the most delicious fish in the world.

Without the advantage of these rivers, whose abundance of waters is almost comparable to an ocean, the plains of Russia would be uninhabitable. Land, land everywhere; an ocean of land, a uniformity of soil, no rocks, no hills, so that stone is almost unknown in Russia. St. Petersburg was the first city not built entirely of wood, and it is an axiom, that Russian houses, as a rule, burn once in seven years. This dulness and desolation of Nature's aspect must of course influence brain and imagination, and consequently must be reflected in the literature, where melancholy predominates even in satire, and whence is derived a tendency to pessimism and a sort of religious devotion tinged with misery and sadness. Indolence, fatalism, inconstancy, — these are the defects of Russian character; resignation, patience, kindness, tolerance, humility, its better qualities. Its passive resignation may be readily transformed into heroism; and Count Léon Tolstoï, in his military narrative of the "Siege of Sevastopol," and his novel "War and Peace," studies and portrays in a wonderful way these traits of the national soul.

IV.

RUSSIAN HISTORY.

History has been for Russia as inclement and hostile as Nature. A cursory glance will suffice to show this, and it is foreign to my purpose to devote more than slight attention to it.

The Greeks, the civilizers of the world, brought their culture to Colchis and became acquainted with the very southernmost parts of Russia known as Sarmatia and Scythia. Herodotus has left us minute descriptions of the inhabitants of the Cimmerian plains, their ways, customs, religions, and superstitions, distinguishing between the industrious Scythians who produce and sell grain, and the nomadic Scythians, the Cossacks, who, depending on their pastures, neither sow nor work. The Sarmatian region was invaded and subjugated by the northern Sclavs, who in turn were conquered by the Goths, these by the Huns, and finally, upon the same field, Huns, Alans, and Bulgarians fought one another for the mastery. In this first confused period there is no historical outline of the Russia that was to be. Her real history begins in a, to us, strange event, whose authenticity historical criticism may question, but which is the basis of all tradition concerning the origin of Russian institutions; I mean the famous message sent by the Sclavs to those Norman or Scandinavian princes, those daring adventurers, the Vikings supposedly (but it matters not), saying to this effect, more or less: "Our land is broad and fertile, but there is neither law nor justice within it; come and possess it and govern it."

Upon the foundation provided by this strange proceeding many very original theories and philosophical conclusions have been built concerning Russian history; and the partisans of autocracy and the ancient order of things consider it a sure evidence that Russia was destined by Heaven to acknowledge an absolute power of foreign derivation, and to bow voluntarily to its saving yoke. Whether the triumphal rulers were Normans or Scandinavians or the original Sclavs, it is certain that with their appearance on the scene as the element of military strength and of disciplined organization, the history of Russia begins : the date of this foreign admixture (which would be for us a day of mourning and shame) Russia to-day celebrates as a glorious millennium. Heroic Russia came into being with the Varangian or Viking chieftains, and it is that age which provides the subject of the *bilinas;* it was the ninth century after Christ, at the very moment when the epic and romantic life of Spain awoke and followed in the train of the Cid.

With the establishment of order and good government among the Sclavs, Rurik founded the nation, as certainly as he founded later the legendary city of Novgorod, and his brother and successor, Olaf, that of Kief, mother of all the Russian cities. It fell to Rurik's race also to give the signal for that secular resistance which even to-day Russia maintains toward her perpetual enemy, Constantinople ; the Russian fleets descended the Dnieper to the Byzantine seas to perish again and again under the Greek fire. Russia received also from this same Byzantium, against which her arms are ever turned, the Christian religion, which was delivered to Olga by Constantine Porfirogenitus. Who shall say what a change there might have been over the face of the earth if the Oriental

Sclavs had received their religion from Rome, like the Poles?

Olga was the Saint Clotilde of Russia; in Vladimir we see her Clodovicus. He was a sensuous and sanguinary barbarian, though at times troubled with religious anxieties, who at the beginning of his reign upheld paganism and revived the worship of idols, at whose feet he sacrificed the Christians. But his darkened conscience was tortured nevertheless by aspirations toward a higher moral light, and he opened a discussion on the subject of the best religion known to mankind. He dismissed Mahometanism because it forbade the use of the red wine which rejoiceth the heart of man; Judaism because its adherents were wanderers over the face of the earth; Catholicism because it was not sufficiently splendid and imposing. His childish and primitive mind was taken with the Asiatic splendors of the church of Constantinople, and being already espoused to the sister of the Byzantine emperor, he returned to his own country bringing its priests with him, cast his old idols into the river, and compelled his astonished vassals to plunge into the same waters and receive baptism perforce, while the divinity he venerated but yesterday was beaten, smeared with blood, and buried ignominiously. Happy the people upon whom the gospel has not been forced by a cruel tyrant, at the point of the sword and under threats of torture, but to whom it has been preached by a humble apostle, the brother of innumerable martyrs and saintly confessors! In the twelfth century, when Christianity inspired us to reconquer our country, Russia, more than half pagan, wept for her idols, and seemed to see them rising from the depths of the river demanding adoration. From this corrupt Byzantine source Russia derived her second civilization, counting as the first that proceeding from the colonization and commerce of the Greeks, as related by Herodotus. The dream of Yaroslaus, the Russian Charlemagne, was to make his capital, Kief, a rival and imitator of Byzantium. From Byzantium came the arts, customs, and ideas; and it seemed the fate of the Sclav race to get the pattern for its intellectual life from abroad.

Some Russian thinkers deem it advantageous for their country to have received its Christianity from Byzantium, and consider it an element of greater independence that the national Church never arrogated to itself the supremacy and dominion over the State. Let such advantages be judged by the rule of autocracy and the nullity of the Greek Church. The Catholic nations, being educated in a more spiritual and exalted idea of liberty, have never allowed that the monarch could be lord of the human conscience, and have never known that monstrous confusion of attributes which makes the sovereign absolute dictator of souls. The Crusade, that fecund movement which was the work of Rome, never spread over Russia; and when the Sclavs fell under the Tartar yoke, the rest of Europe left her to her fate. Russia's choice of this branch of the Christian religion was fatal to her dominion over other kindred Sclavs; for it embittered her rivalry with the Poles, and raised an insurmountable barrier between Russia and European civilization which was inseparably intertwined with the Catholic faith even in such phenomena as the Renaissance, which seems at first glance laic and pagan.

Nevertheless, so much of Christianity as fell to Russia through the accepted channel sufficed to open to her the doors of the civilized world, and to rouse her from the torpid sleep of the Oriental. It gave her the rational and proper form of family life as indicated by monogamy, whose early adoption is one of the highest and most distinguishing marks of the Aryan race ; and instead of the savage chieftain surrounded by his fierce vassals always ready for rebellion and bloodshedding, it gave the idea of a monarch who lives as God's vicar upon the earth, the living incarnation of law and order, — an idea which, in times of anarchy and confusion, served to constitute the State and establish it upon a firm basis. Lastly, Russia owes to Christianity her ecclesiastical literature, the fount and origin of literary culture throughout Europe.

In the thirteenth century — that bright and luminous age, the time of Saint Thomas, of Saint Francis of Assisi, of Dante, of Saint Ferdinand — Russia was suddenly invaded by the Mongols, and, like locusts in a corn-field, those hideous and demoniacal foes fell upon her and made all Christendom tremble, so that the French historian Joinville records it as a sign of the coming of Antichrist. " For our sins the unknown nations covered our land," say the Russian chroniclers. Genghis Khan, after subduing all Asia, drew around him an immense number of tribes, and fell upon Russia with irresistible force, sowing the land with skulls as the flower of the field sows it with seeds, and compelling the once free and wealthy native Boyars to bring grist to the mill and serve their conquerors as slaves. The Russian towns and princes performed miracles of heroism, but in vain. The Tartar hordes, let loose upon those vast plains where their horses found abundant pasture, rolled over the land like an inundation. In a more varied country, more densely populated and with better communication, the Tartars would have been beaten back, as they were from Moravia. Again Nature's hand was upon the destinies of Russia; the topographical conditions laid her under the power of the Golden Horde.

This great misfortune not only isolated Russia from the Occident and left her under Asiatic sway, but it also subjugated her to the growing autocracy of the Muscovite princes who were becoming formidable oppressors of their subjects, and they in turn were victims, tributaries, and vassals of the great Khans. So the invasion came to exercise a decisive influence upon the institutions of the future empire, pernicious in consequence of the abnormal development allowed to monarchical authority, and beneficent inasmuch as it aided forcibly in the formation of the nationality. At the time of the Mongol irruption Russia was composed of various independent principalities governed by the descendants of Rurik; the necessity of opposing the invader demonstrated the necessity also of uniting all under one sceptre.

Continually chafing at the bit, dissimulating and temporizing with the enemy by means of clever diplomatic envoys, the princes slowly cemented their power and prepared the land for a homogeneous state, until one day the chivalrous Donskoi, the victor at the battle of the Don, opened the era of reconquest, exclaiming in the exuberance of his first triumph over the Tartars, "Their day is past, and God is with us!" But Russia's evil star awoke one of the greatest captains named in history, Tamerlane, who ruined the work begun by Donskoï, and toward the end of the fourteenth century once more laid the Muscovite people under subjection.

At the meeting of the Council of Florence, when the Greek Emperor John Paleologos agreed to the reunion of the two churches, the prince of Moscow, Basil the Blind, showed himself blind of soul as well as of eye, in obstinately opposing such a union, thus cutting off Russia again from the Occident. When the Turks took Constantinople and consummated the fall of the Byzantine empire, Moscow became the capital of the Greek world, the last bulwark of the schismatic church, the asylum of the remains of a depraved and perishing organism, of the senile decadence of the last of the Cæsars.

V.

THE RUSSIAN AUTOCRACY.

SUCH was the sad situation in Russia at the opening of the period of European Renaissance, out of which grew the modern age which was to provide the remedy for her ills through her own tyrants. For without intending a paradox, I will say that tyranny is the liberator of Russia. Twice these tyrants who have forced life into her, who have impelled her toward the future, have been called *The Terrible*, — Ivan III., the uniter of the provinces, he whose very look made the women faint, and Ivan IV., the first to use the title of Czar. Both these despots cross the stage of history like spectres called up by a nightmare : the former morose, dissimulating, and hypocritical, like Louis XI. of France, whom he resembles; the latter demented, fanatical, epileptic, and hot-tempered, clutching his iron pike in hand, with which he transfixed Russia as one may transfix a fluttering insect with a pin. But these tyrants, gifted and guided by a saving instinct, created the nation. Ivan III. instituted the succession to the throne, thus suppressing the hurtful practice of partition among brothers, and it was he who finally broke the yoke of the Mongols. Ivan IV. did more yet; he achieved the actual separation of Europe from Asia, put down the anarchy of the nobles, and taught them submission to law; and not content with this, he put himself at the head of the scanty literature of his time, and while he widened the domains of Russia, he protected within her borders the establishment of the press, until then persecuted as sacrilegious. It is difficult to think what would have become of the Russian nation without her great tyrants. Therefore it is that the memory of Ivan IV. still lives in the popular imagination, and the Terrible Czar, like Pedro the Cruel of Spain, is neither forgotten nor abhorred.

The consolidation of the autocratic idea is easily understood in the light of these historic figures. No wonder that the people accepted it, from a spirit of self-preservation, since it was despotism that sustained them, that formed them, so to speak. It is folly to consider the institutions of a nation as though they were extraneous to it, fruit of an individual will or of a single event; society obeys laws as exact as those which regulate the courses of the stars, and the historian must recognize and fix them.

The autocracy and the unity of Russia were consolidated together by the genius of Ivan III., who made their emblem the double-headed eagle, and by Ivan IV., who sacrificed to them a sea of blood. The municipal autonomies and the petty independent princes frowned, but Russia became a true nation; at the beginning of the sixteenth century, the brilliant age of the monarchical principle, no European sovereign could boast of being so thoroughly obeyed as the sovereign prince of Moscow.

The radical concept of omnipotent power, not tempered as in the West by the humanity of Catholicism, at once rushed headlong to oppression and slavery. The ambitious regent Boris Godonoff was not long in attaching the serfs to the soil, and upon the heels of this unscrupulous act followed the dark and bloody days of the false Demetrii, in which the serf, irritated by the burden of his chains, welcomed, in every adventurer, in every impostor, a Messiah come to redeem him. Then the Poles, the eternal enemies of Russia, seized the Kremlin, the Swedes threatened to overcome her, and the nation seemed ready to perish had it not been for the heroism of a butcher and a prince; a suggestive example of the saving strength which at supreme moments rises up in every nation.

But one more providential tyrant was needed, the greatest of all, the most extraordinary man of Russia's history, of the house of Romanoff, successor to the extinct dynasty of the Terrible Ivans. "Terrible" might also be applied to the name of the imperial carpenter whose character and destiny are not unlike those of Ivan IV. Both were precocious in intellect, both were self-educated, and both cooled their hot youth in the hard school of abandonment. Out of it came Peter the Great, determined at all costs to remodel his gigantic empire.

Herodotus relates how the young Anacarsis, on returning from foreign lands wherein he had learned new arts and sciences, came to Scythia his native country, and wished to celebrate there a great feast, after the manner of the Greeks, in honor of the mother of the gods; hearing of which the king Sarillius impaled him with a lance. He tells also how another king who wearied of the Scythian mode of living, and craved the customs of the Greeks, among whom he had been educated, endeavored to introduce the Bacchanalian dances, himself taking part in them. The Scythians refused to conform to these novel ideas, and finally cut off the king's head; for, adds the historian, "The Scythians detest nothing so much as foreign customs." The tale of Herodotus was in danger of being repeated at the beginning of the reign of Peter Romanoff. With him began the battle, not yet ended, between old Russia, which calls itself Holy, and new Russia, cut after the Western pattern. While Peter travelled and studied the industry and progress of Europe with the idea of bringing them to his Byzantine empire, the rebels at home conspired to dethrone this daring innovator who threatened to use fire and sword, whips and scourges, the very implements of barbarism, against barbarism itself.

It is a notable fact in Russian history that none of her mighty sovereigns was possessed of moral conditions in harmony with the vigor of their intelligence and will force. Russia has had great emperors but not good emperors. The halo that wreathes the head of Berenguela of Castile and Isabel the Catholic, Saint Ferdinand, or Saint Louis, — men and women in whom the ideal of justice seemed to become incarnate, — is lacking to Vladimir the Baptizer, to Ivan IV., to Peter the Great. Among Occidental peoples the monarchy owed its prestige and sacred authority to good and just kings, vicars of God on earth, who were impressed with a sense of being called to play a noble part in the drama of history, conscious of grave responsibilities, and sure of having to render an account of their stewardship to a Supreme Power. The Czars present quite a different aspect: they seem to have understood civilization rather by its externals than by its intrinsic doctrines, which demand first of all our inward perfecting, our gradual elevation above the level of the beast, and the continuous affirmation of our dignity. Therefore they used material force as their instrument, and spared no means to crown their efforts.

But with all it is impossible to withhold a tribute of admiration to Peter the Great. That fierce despot, gross and vicious, was not only a reformer but a hero. Pultowa, which beheld the fall of the power of Sweden, justified the reforms and the military organization instituted by the young emperor, and made Russia a European power,—a power respected, influential, and great. Whatever may be said against war, whatever sentimental comparisons may be made between the founder and the conqueror, it must still be admitted that the monarch who leads his people to victory will lead them *ipse facto* to new destinies, to a more glorious and intense historic life.

If Peter the Great had vacillated one degree, if he had squandered time and opportunity in studying prudent ways and means for planting his reforms, if his hand had trembled in laying the rod across the backs of his nobles, or had spared the lash upon the flesh of his own son, perhaps he would never have achieved the transformation of his Oriental empire into a European State, a transformation which embraced everything, — the navy, the army, public instruction, social relations, commerce, customs, and even the beards of his subjects, the much respected traditional long beards, mercilessly shaven by order of the autocrat. In his zeal for illimitable authority, and that his decrees might meet with no obstacles either in heaven or earth, this Czar conceived the bright idea of assuming the spiritual power, and having suppressed the Patriarchy and created the Synod, he held in his hands the conscience of his people, could count its every pulsation, and wind it up like a well-regulated clock. What considerations, human or divine, will check a man who, like Abraham, sacrifices his first-born to an idea, and makes himself the executioner of his own son?

The race sign was not obliterated from the Russian culture produced by immoral and short-sighted reformers. A woman of low extraction and obscure history, elevated to the imperial purple, was the one to continue the work of Peter the Great; his daughter's favorite became the protector of public instruction and the founder of the University of Moscow; a frivolous and dissolute Czarina, Elisabeth Petrowna, modified the customs, encouraged intellectual pleasures and dramatic representations, and put Russia in contact with the Latin mind as developed in France; another empress, a parricide, a usurper and libertine, who deserves the perhaps pedantic name of the Semiramis of the North given her by Voltaire, hid her delinquencies under the splendor of her intellect, the refined delicacy of her artistic tastes, her gifts as a writer, and her magnificence as a sovereign.

It was the profound and violent shock administered by the hard hand of Peter the Great that impelled Russia along the road to French culture, and with equal violence she retraced her steps at the invasion of the armies of Napoleon. The nobility and the patriots of Russia cursed France in French, — the language which had been taught them as the medium of progress; and the nation became conscious of its own individuality in the hour of trial, in the sudden awakening of its independent instincts. But in proportion as the nationality arose in its might, the low murmur of a growing revolution made itself heard. This impulse did not burst first from the hearts of the people, ground down by the patriarchal despotism of Old Russia, but from the brain of the educated classes, especially the nobility. The first sign of the strife, predestined from the close of the war with the French, was the political repression of the last years of the reign of Alexander I., and the famous republican conspiracy of December against Nicholas, — an aristocratic outbreak contrived by men in whose veins ran the blood of princes. Of these events I shall speak more fully when I come to the subject of Nihilism; I merely mention it here in this general glimpse of Russian history.

Menaced by Asia, Russia had willingly submitted to an absolute power, because, as we have seen, she lacked the elements that had concurred in the formation of modern Europe. Classic civilization never entered her veins; she had no other light than that which shone from Byzantium, nor any other model than that offered by the later empire; she had no place in the great Catholic fraternity which had its law and its focus in Rome, and the Mongolian invasion accomplished her complete isolation. Spain also suffered an invasion of a foreign race, but she pulled herself together and sustained herself on a war-footing for seven centuries. Russia could not do this, but bent her neck to the yoke of the conqueror. Our national character would have chafed indeed to see the kings of Asturias and Castile, instead of perpetually challenging the Moors, become their humble vassals, as the Muscovite princes were to the Khans. With us the struggle for re-conquest, far from exhausting us, redoubled our thirst for independence, — a thirst born farther back than that time, in spite of Leroy-Beaulieu's statement, although it was indeed confirmed and augmented during the progress of that Hispano-Saracenic Iliad. The Russians being obliged to lay down their arms, to suffer and to wait, assumed, instead of our ungovernable vehemence, a patient resignation. But they none the less considered themselves a nation, and entertained a hope of vindicating their rights, which they accomplished finally in the overthrow of the Tartars, and in later days in rising against the French with an impetuosity and spontaneity almost as savage as Spain had shown in her memorable days. Moreover, Russia lacked the elements of historic activity necessary to enable her to play an early part in the work of modern civilization. She had no feudalism, no nobility (as we understand the term), no chivalry, no Gothic architecture, no troubadours, no knights. She lacked the intellectual impetus of mediæval courts, the sturdy exercise of scholastic disputations, the elucidations of the problems of the human race, which were propounded by the thirteenth century. She lacked the religious orders, that network which enclosed the wide edifice of Catholicism; and the military, uniting in mystic sympathy the ascetic and chivalric sentiments. She lacked the councils of the laws of modern rights; and that her lack might be in nothing lacking, she lacked even the brilliant heresies of the West, the subtle rationalists and pantheists, the Abelards and Amalrics, whose followers were brilliant ignoramuses or rank bigots roused by a question of ritual. Lastly, she lacked the sunny smile of Pallas Athene and the Graces, the Renaissance, which brightened the face of Europe at the close of the Middle Ages.

And as the civilization brought at last to Russia was the product of nations possessed of all that Russia lacked, and as finally, it was imposed upon her by force, and without those gradual transitions and insensible modifications as necessary to a people as to an individual, she could not accept it in the frank and cordial manner indispensable to its beneficent action. A nation which receives a culture ready made, and not elaborated by itself, condemns itself to intellectual sterility; at most it can only hope to imitate well. And so it happened with Russia. Her development does not present the continuous bent, the gentle undulations of European history in which yesterday creates to-day, and to-day prepares for to-morrow, without an irregular or awkward halt, or ever a trace broken. In the social order of Russia primitive institutions coexist with products of our spick and span new sociology, and we see the deep waters of the past mixed with the froth of the Utopia that points out the route of the unknown future. This confusion or inharmoniousness engenders Russian dualism, the cause of her political and moral disturbances. Russia contains an ancient people, to-day an anachronism, and a society in embryo struggling to burst its bounds.

But above all it is evident there is a people eager to speak, to come forth, to have a weight in the world, because its long-deferred time has come; a race which, from an insignificant tribe mewed in around the sources of the Dnieper, has spread out into an immense nation, whose territory reaches from the Baltic to the Pacific, from the Arctic to the borders of Turkey, Persia, and China; a nation which has triumphed over Sweden, Poland, the Turks, the Mongols, and the French; a nation by nature expansive, colonizing, mighty in extent, most interesting in the qualities of the genius it is developing day by day, and which is more astonishing than its material greatness, because it is the privilege of intellect to eclipse force. Half a dozen brains and spirits who are now spelling out their race for us, arrest and captivate all who contemplate this great empire. Out of the poverty of traditions and institutions which Russian history bewails, two characteristic ones appear as bases of national life: the autocracy, and the agrarian commune, — absolute imperial power and popular democracy.

The geography of Russia, which predisposes her both to unity and to invasion, which obliges her to concentrate herself, and to seek in a vigorous autocratic principle the consciousness of independent being as a people, created the formidable dominion of the Muscovite Czars, which has no equal in the world. Like all primordial Russian ideas, the plan of this Cæsarian sovereignty proceeded from Byzantium, and was founded by Greek refugee priests, who surrounded it with the aureole of divinity indispensable to the establishment of advantageous superstitions so fecund in historical results. Since the twelfth century the autocracy has been a fixed fact, and has gone on assuming all the prerogatives, absorbing all the power, and symbolizing in the person of one man this colossal nation. The sovereign princes, discerning clearly the object and end of these aims, have spared no means to attain to it. They began by checking the proud Boyars in their train, reducing them from companions and equals to subjects; later on they devoted themselves to the suppression of all institutions of democratic character.

For the sake of those who judge of a race by the political forms it uses, it should be observed that Russia has not only preserved latent in her the spirit of democracy, but that she possessed in the Middle Ages republican institutions more liberal and radical than any in the rest of Europe. The Italian republics, which at bottom were really oligarchies, cannot compare with the municipal and communist republics of Viatka, Pskof, and especially the great city of Novgorod, which called itself with pride Lord Novgorod the Great. The supreme power there resided in an assembly of the citizens; the prince was content to be an administrator or president elected by free suffrage, and above all an ever-ready captain in time of war; on taking his office he swore solemnly to respect the laws, customs, and privileges of the republic; if he committed a perjury, the assembly convened in the public square at the clang of an ancient bell, and the prince, having been declared a traitor, was stripped, expelled, and *cast into the mud*, according to the forcible popular expression. This industrious republic reached the acme of its prosperity in the thirteenth and fourteenth centuries, after which the rising principality of Moscow, now sure of its future, came and took down the bells of Novgorod the Great, and so silenced their voices of bronze and the voice of Russian liberties, though not without a bloody battle, as witnesseth the whirlpool — which is still pointed out to the curious traveller — under the bridge of the ancient republican city, whose inhabitants were drowned there by Ivan the Terrible. Upon their dead bodies he founded the unity of the empire. Nor are the free towns the only tradition of autonomy which disturbed the growing autocratic power. The Cossacks for a long time formed an independent and warlike aristocracy, proud and indomitable; and to subdue and incorporate these bellicose tribes with the rest of the nation it was necessary to employ both skill and force.

We may say without vanity that although the Spaniards exalted monarchical loyalty into a cult, they never depreciated human dignity. Amongst us the king is he who makes right (*face derecho*), and if he makes it not, we consider him a tyrant, a usurper of the royal prerogative; in acknowledging him lord of life and property, we protest (by the mouth of Calderon's honest rustic) against the idea that he can arrogate to himself also the dominion over conscience and soul; and the smallest subject in Spain would not endure at the king's hand the blows administered by Peter the Great for the correction of his nobles, themselves descendants of Rurik. In Russia, where the inequalities and extremes of climate seem to have been communicated to its institutions, there was nothing between the independent republics and the autocracy. In Spain, the slightest territorial disaffection, the fruit of partial conquests or insignificant victories, was an excuse for some upstart princeling, our instinctive tendencies being always monarchical and anything like absolute authority and Cæsarism, so odious that we never allowed it even in our most excellent kings; a dream of imperial power would almost have cost them the throne. In Russia, absolutism is in the air, — one sole master, one lord omnipotent, the image of God himself.

Read the Muscovite code. The Czar is named therein *the autocrat whose power is unlimited*. See the catechism which is taught in the schools of Poland; it says that the subject owes to the Czar, not love or loyalty, but adoration. Hear the Russian hymn; amid its harmonies the same idea resounds. In all the common forms of salutation to the Czar we shall find something that excites in us a feeling of rebellion, something that represents us as unworthy to stand before him as one mortal before another. Paul I. said to a distinguished foreigner, "You must know that in Russia there is no person more important than the person to whom I speak and while I speak." A Czar who directs by means of *ukases* not only the dress but even the words of the language which his subjects must use, and changes the track of a railroad by a stroke of his pen, frightens one even more than when he signs a sentence of proscription; for he reaches the high-water mark of authority when he interferes in these simple and unimportant matters, and demonstrates what one may call the micrography of despotism. If anything can excuse or even commend to our eyes this obedience carried to an absurdity, it is its paternal character. There are no offences between fathers and sons, and the Czar never can insult a subject. The serf calls him *thou* and *Father*, and on seeing him pass he takes off his cap though the snow falls, crossing his hands over his breast with religious veneration. For him the Czar possesses every virtue, and is moved only by the highest purposes; he thinks him impeccable, sacred, almost immortal. If we abide by the judgment of those who see a symbol of the Russian character in the call of Rurik and the voluntary placing of the power in his hands, the autocracy will not seem a secular abuse or a violent tyranny, but rather an organic product of a soil and a race; and it will inspire the respect drawn forth by any spontaneous and genuine production.

There exists in Russia a small school of thinkers on public affairs, important by reason of the weight they have had and still have upon public opinion. They are called Sclavophiles, — people enamoured of their ancient land, who affirm that the essence of Russian nationality is to be found in the customs and institutions of the laboring classes who are not contaminated by the artificial civilization imported from the corrupt West; who make a point of appearing on occasions in the national dress, — the red silk blouse and velvet jacket, the long beard and the clumsy boots. According to them, the only independent forces on which Russia can count are the people and the Czar, — the immense herd of peasants, and, at the top, the autocrat. And in fact the Russian empire, in spite of official hierarchies, is a rural state in which the sentiment of democratic equality predominates so entirely that the people, not content with having but yesterday taken the Czar's part against the rich and mighty Boyars, sustains him to-day against the revolution, loves him, and cannot conceive of intermediaries between him and his subjects, between lord and vassal, or, to put it still more truly, between father and son. And having once reduced the nobles, with the consent of the people, to the condition of inoffensive hangers-on of the court, many thinkers believe that the Czar need only lean upon the rude hand of the peasant to quell whatever political disaffection may arise. So illimitable is the imperial power, that it becomes impotent against itself if it would reduce itself by relegating any of its influence to a class, such as, for instance, the aristocracy. If turbulent magnates or sullen conspirators manage to get rid of the person of the Czar, the principle still remains inviolate.

VI.

THE AGRARIAN COMMUNES.

At the right hand of the imperial power stands the second Russian national institution, the municipal commune known as the *mir*, which is arresting the attention of European statesmen and sociologists, since they have learned of its existence (thanks to the work of Baron Haxsthausen on the internal life of Russia). Who is not astonished at finding realized in the land of the despots a large number of the communist theories which are the terror of the middle classes in liberal countries, and various problems, of the kind we call formidable, there practically solved? And why should not a nation often called barbarous swell with pride at finding itself, suddenly and without noise or effort, safely beyond what in others threatens the extremity of social revolution? Therefore it happens that since the discovery of the *mir*, the Russians have one argument more, and not a weak one, against the corrupt civilization of the Occident. The European nations, they say, are running wildly toward anarchy, and in some, as England, the concentration of property in a few hands creates a proletariat a thousand times more unhappy than the Russian serf ever was, a hungry horde hostile to the State and to the wealthy classes. Russia evades this danger by means of the *mir*. In the Russian village the land belongs to the municipality, amongst whose members it is distributed periodically; each able-bodied individual receives what he needs, and is spared hunger and disgrace.

Foreigners have not been slow to examine into the advantages of such an arrangement. Mackenzie Wallace has pronounced it to be truly constitutional, as the phrase is understood in his country; not meaning a sterile and delusive law, written upon much paper and enwrapped in formulas, but a traditional concept which came forth at the bidding of real and positive necessities. What an eloquent lesson for those who think they have improved upon the plan of the ages! History, scouting our thirst for progress, offers us again in the *mir* the picture of the serpent biting his own tail. This institution, so much lauded by the astonished traveller and the meditative philosopher, is really a sociological fossil, remains of prehistoric times, preserved in Russia by reason of the suspension or slow development of the history of the race. Students of law have told me that in the ancient forms of Castilian realty, those of Santander, for example, there have been discovered traces of conditions analogous to the Russian *mir*. And when I have seen the peasants of my own province assembled in the church-porch after Mass, I have imagined I could see the remains of this Saturnian and patriarchal type of communist partition. Common possession of the land is a primitive idea as remote as the prehistoric ages; it belongs to the paleontology of social science, and in those countries where civilization early flourished, gave way before individual interest and the modern idea of property. "Happy age and blessed times were those," exclaimed Don Quixote, looking at a handful of acorns, "which the ancients called golden, and not because gold which in our iron age has such a value set on it, not because gold could be got without any trouble, but because those who lived in it were ignorant of those two words, *mine* and *thine!* In that blessed age everything was in common; nobody needed to take any more trouble for his necessities than to stretch forth his hand and take from the great oak-trees the sweet and savory fruit so liberally offered!" Gone long ago for us is the time deplored by the ingenious knight, but it has reappeared there in the North, where, according to our information, it is still recent; for it is thought that the *mir* was established about the sixteenth century.

The character of the *mir* is entirely democratic; the oldest peasant represents the executive power in the municipal assembly, but the authority resides in the assembly itself, which consists of all the heads of families, and convenes Sundays in the open air, in the public square or the church-porch. The assembly wields a sacred power which no one disputes. Next to the Czar the Russian peasant loves his *mir*, among whose members the land is in common, as also the lake, the mills, the canals, the flocks, the granary, the forest. It is all re-divided from time to time, in order to avoid exclusive appropriation. Half the cultivable land in the empire is subject to this system, and no capitalist or land-owner can disturb it by acquiring even an inch of municipal territory; the laborer is born invested with the right of possession as certainly as we are all entitled to a grave. In spite of a feeling of distrust and antipathy against communism, and of my own ignorance in these matters which precludes my judgment of them, I must confess to a certain agreement with the ardent apologists of the Russian agrarian municipality. Tikomirov says that in Russia individual and collective property-rights still quarrel, but that the latter has the upper hand; this seems strange, since the modern tendency is decidedly toward individualism, and it is hard to conceive of a return to patriarchal forms; but there is no reason to doubt the vitality of the *mir* and its generation and growth in the heart of the fatherland, and this is certainly worthy of note, especially in a country like Russia, so much given to the imitation of foreign models. Mere existence and permanence is no *raison d'être* for any institution, for many exist which are pernicious and abominable; but when an institution is found to be in harmony with the spirit of the people, it must have a true merit and value. It is said that the tendency to aggregate, either in agrarian municipalities or in trades guilds and corporations, is born in the blood and bred in the bone of the Sclavs, and that they carry out these associations wherever they go, by instinct, as the bee makes its cells always the same; and it is certainly true that as an ethnic force the communistic principle claims a right to develop itself in Russia. It is certain that the *mir* fosters in the poor Russian village habits of autonomous administration and municipal liberty, and that in the shadow of this humble and primitive institution men have found a common home within the fatherland, no matter how scattered over its vast plains. "The heavens are very high, and the Czar is far off," says the Russian peasant sadly, when he is the victim of any injustice; his only refuge is the *mir*, which is always close at hand. The *mir* acts also as a counterbalance to a centralized administration, which is an inevitable consequence of the conformation of Russian territory; and it creates an advantageous solidarity among the farmers, who are equal owners of the same heritages and subject to the same taxes.

Since 1861 the rural governments, released from all seignorial obligations, elect their officers from among themselves, and the smaller municipal groups, still preserving each its own autonomy, meet together in one larger municipal body called *volost*, which corresponds to the better-known term *canton*. No institution could be more democratic : here the laboring man discusses his affairs *en famille*, without interference from other social classes; the *mir* boasts of it, as also of the fact that it has never in its corporate existence known head or chief, even when its members were all serfs. In fine, the *mir* holds its sessions without any presiding officer; rooted in the communist and equal-rights idea, it acknowleges no law of superiority; it votes by unanimous acclamation; the minority yields always to the general opinion, to oppose which would be thought base obstinacy. "Only God shall judge the *mir*," says the proverb; the word *mir*, say the etymological students and admirers of the institution, means, "world," "universe," "complete and perfect microcosm," which is sufficient unto itself and is governed by its own powers.

To what does the *mir* owe its vitality? To the fact that it did not originate in the mind of the Utopian or the ideologist, but was produced naturally by derivation from the family, from which type the whole Russian state organization springs. It should be understood, however, that the peasant family in Russia differs from our conception of the institution, recalling as it does, like all purely Russian institutions, the most ancient or prehistoric forms. The family, or to express it in the language of the best writers on the subject, the *great Russian family*, is an association of members submitted to the absolute authority of the eldest, generally the grandfather, — a fact personally interesting to me because of the surprising resemblance it discloses between Russia and the province of Gallicia, where I perceive traces of this family power in the *petrucios*, or elders. In this association everything is in common, and each individual works for all the others. To the head of the house is given a name which may be translated as administrator, major-domo, or director of works, but conveys no idea of relationship. The laws of inheritance and succession are understood in the same spirit, and very differently from our custom. When a house or an estate is to be settled, the degree of relationship among the heirs is not considered; the whole property is divided equally between the male adults, including natural or adopted sons if they have served in the family the same as legitimate sons, while the married daughter is considered as belonging to the family of her husband, and she and the son who has separated himself from the parent house are excluded from the succession, or rather from the final liquidation or settlement between the associates. Although there is a law of inheritance written in the Russian Code, it is a dead letter to a people opposed to the idea of individual property.

Intimately connected with this communist manner of interpreting the rights of inheritance and succession are certain facts in Russian history. For a long time the sovereign authority was divided among the sons of the ruler; and as the Russian nobility rebelled against the establishment of differences founded upon priority in birth, entail and primogeniture took root with difficulty, in spite of the efforts made by the emperors to import Occidental forms of law. Their idea of succession is so characteristic that, like the Goths, they sometimes prefer the collateral to the immediate branch, and the brother instead of the son will mount the steps of the throne. It is important to note these radical differences, because a race which follows an original method in the matter of its laws has a great advantage in setting out upon genuine literary creations.

But while the family, understood as a group or an association, offers many advantages from the agrarian point of view, its disadvantages are serious and considerable because it annuls individual liberty. It facilitates agricultural labors, it puts a certain portion of land at the service of each adult member, as well as tools, implements, fuel, and cattle; helps each to a maintenance; precludes hunger; avoids legal exactions (for the associated family cannot be taxed, just as the *mir* cannot be deprived of its lands); but on the other hand it puts the individual, or rather the true family, the human pair, under an intolerable domestic tyranny. According to traditional usage, the authority of the head of the family was omnipotent: he ordered his house, as says an old proverb, like a Khan of the Crimea; his gray hairs were sacred, and he wielded the power of a tribal chieftain rather than of a head of a house. In our part of the world marriage emancipates; in Russia, it was the first link in a galling chain. The oppression lay heaviest upon the woman: popular songs recount the sorrows of the daughters-in-law subjected to the maltreatment of mothers-in-law and sisters-in-law, or the victims of the vicious appetites of the chief, who in a literally Biblical spirit thought himself lord of all that dwelt beneath his roof. Truly those institutions which sometimes elicit our admiration for their patriarchal simplicity hide untold iniquities, and develop a tendency to the abuse of power which seems inherent in the human species.

At first sight nothing could be more attractive than the great Russian family, nothing more useful than the rural communes; and nowadays, when we are applying the laws and technicism of physiology to the study of society, this primordial association would seem the cell from which the true organism of the State may be born; the family is a sort of lesser municipality, the municipality is a larger family, and the whole Russian people is an immense agglomeration, a great ant-hill whose head is the emperor. In the popular songs we see the Oriental idea of the nation expressed as the family, when the peasant calls the Czar *father*. But this primitive machinery can never prevail against the notion of individualism entertained among civilized peoples. Our way of understanding property, which the admirers of the Russian commune consider fundamentally vicious, is the only way compatible with the independence and dignity of work and the development of industries and arts. The Russian *mir* may prevent the growth of the proletariat, but it is by putting mankind in bonds. It may be said that agrarian communism only differs from servitude in that the latter provides one master and the former many; and that though the laboring man theoretically considers himself a member of a co-operative agricultural society, he is in reality a slave, subject to collective responsibilities and obligations, by virtue of which he is tied to the soil the same as the vassals of our feudal epochs. Perhaps the new social conditions which are the fruit of the emancipation of the serfs, which struck at and violated the great associated family, will at last undermine the *mir*, unless the *mir* learns some way to adapt itself to any political mutations. What is most important to the study of the historical development and the social ideas as shown in modern Russian literature, is to understand how by means of the great family and the agrarian municipality, communism and socialism run in the veins of the people of Russia, so that Leroy-Beaulieu could say with good reason, that if they are to be preserved from the pernicious effects of the Occidental proletariat it must be by inoculation, as vaccination exempts from small-pox.

The socialist leaven may be fairly said to lie in the most important class in the Russian State, — important not alone by reason of numerical superiority, but because it is the depositary of the liveliest national energies and the custodian of the future: I mean the peasants. There are some who think that this *mujik*, this *little man* or *black man*, tiller of still blacker soil, holds the future destinies of Europe in his hands; and that when this great new Horde becomes conscious some day of its strength and homogeneity, it will rise, and in its concentrated might fall upon some portion of the globe, and there will be no defence or resistance possible. In the rest of Europe it is the cities, the urban element, which regulates the march of political events. Certainly Spain is not ignorant of this fact, since she has a vivid remembrance of civil wars in which the rustic element, representing tradition, was vanquished. In Russia, the cities have no proportionate influence, and that which demands the special attention of the governor or the revolutionist is the existence, needs, and thoughts of the innumerable peasant communities, who are the foundation and material of an empire justly termed rural. From this is derived a sort of cult, an apotheosis which is among the most curious to be found in Russian modern literature. Of the peasant, wrapped in badly cured sheepskins, and smelling like a beast; the humble and submissive peasant, yesterday laden with the chains of servitude; the dirty, cabbage-eating peasant, drunk with *wodka,* who beats his wife and trembles with fright at ghosts, at the Devil, and at thunder, — of this peasant, the charity of his friends and the poetic imagination of Russian writers has made a demi-god, an ideal. So great is the power of genius, that without detriment to the claims of truth, picturing him with accurate and even brutal realism (which we shall find native to the Russian novel), Russian authors have distilled from this peasant a poetic essence which we inhale involuntarily until we, aristocratic by instinct, disdainful of the rustic, given to ridicule the garlic-smelling herd, yield to its power. And not content with seeing in this peasant a brother, a neighbor, whom, according to the word of Christ, we ought to love and succor, Russian literature discovers in him a certain indefinable sublimity, a mysterious illumination which other social classes have not. Not merely because of the introduction of the picturesque element in the description of popular customs has it been said that Russian contemporary literature smells of the peasant, but far rather because it raises the peasant to the heights of human moral grandeur, marks in him every virtue, and presupposes him possessed of powers which he never puts forth. From Turguenief, fine poet as he is, to Chtchédrine, the biting satirist, all paint the peasant with loving touch, always find a ready excuse for his defects, and lend him rare qualities, without ever failing to show faithfully his true physiognomy. Corruption, effeminacy, and vice characterize the upper classes, particularly the employées of government, or any persons charged with public trusts; and to make these the more odious, they are attributed with a detestable hypocrisy made more hateful by apparent kindliness and culture.

There is a humorous little novel by Chtchédrine (an author who merits especial mention) entitled

"The Generals[1] and the *Mujik*," which represents two generals of the most ostentatious sort, transported to a desert island, unable either to get food or to get away, until they meet with a *mujik*, who performs all sorts of services for them, even to *making broth in the hollow of his hand*, and then, after making a raft, conveys them safely to St. Petersburg; whereupon these knavish generals, after recovering back pay, send to their deliverer a glass of whiskey and a sum amounting to about three cents. But this bitter allegory is a mild one compared with the mystical apotheosis of the *mujik* as conceived by Tolstoï. In one of his works, "War and Peace," the hero, after seeking vainly by every imaginable means to understand all human wisdom and divine revelation, finds at last the sum of it in a common soldier, imperturbable and dull of soul, and poor in spirit, a prisoner of the French, who endures with calm resignation ill treatment and death without once entertaining the idea of taking the life of his foreign captors. This poor fellow, who, owing to his rude, uncouth mode of life, suffers persecution by other

---

[1] Voguié explains this title of "General" to be both in the civil and military order with the qualification of "Excellency." Without living in Russia one can hardly understand the prestige attached to this title, or the facilities it gives everywhere for everything. To attain this dignity is the supreme ambition of all the servants of the State. The common salutation by way of pleasantry among friends is this line from the comedy of Griboïedof, which has become a proverb: "I wish you health and the *tchin* of a General." — TR.

importunate lesser enemies which I forbear to name, is the one to teach Pierre Besukoff the alpha and omega of all philosophy, wherein he is wise by intuition, and, in virtue of his condition as the peasant, fatalistic and docile.

I have had the good fortune to see with my own eyes this idol of Russian literature, and to satisfy a part of my curiosity concerning some features of Holy Russia. Twenty or thirty peasants from Smolensk who had been bitten by a rabid wolf were sent to Paris to be treated by M. Pasteur. In company with some Russian friends I went to a small hotel, mounted to the fourth floor, and entered a narrow sleeping apartment. The air being breathed by ten or twelve human beings was scarcely endurable, and the fumes of carbolic acid failed to purify it; but while my companions were talking with their compatriots, and a Russian young-lady medical student dressed their wounds, I studied to my heart's content these men from a distant land. I frankly confess that they made a profound impression upon me which I can only describe by saying that they seemed to me like Biblical personages. It gave me a certain pleasure to see in them the marks of an ancient people, rude and rough in outward appearance, but with something majestic and monumental about them, and yet with a suggestion of latent juvenility, the grave and religious air of dreamer or seer, different from really Oriental peoples. Their features, as well as their limbs (which bearing the marks of the wild beast's teeth they held out to be washed and dressed with tranquil resignation), were large and mighty like a tree. One old man took my attention particularly, because he presented a type of the patriarchs of old, and might have served the painter as a model for Abraham or Job, — a wide skull bald at the top, fringed about with yellowish white hair like a halo; a long beard streaked with white also; well-cut features, frontal development very prominent, his eyes half hidden beneath bushy eyebrows. The arm which he uncovered was like an old tree-trunk, rough and knotty, the thick sinuous network of veins reminding one of the roots; his enormous hands, wrinkled and horny, bespoke a life of toil, of incessant activity, of daily strife with the energies of Mother Nature. I heard with delight, though without understanding a word, their guttural speech, musical and harmonious withal, and I needed not to heat my imagination overmuch to see in those poor peasants the realization of the great novelists' descriptions, and an expression of patience and sadness which raised them above vulgarity and coarseness. The sadness may have been the result of their unhappy situation; nevertheless it seemed sweet and poetic.

The attraction which *the people* exercises upon refined and cultivated minds is not surprising. Who has not sometimes experienced with terrible keenness what may be called the æsthetic effect of collectivity? A regiment forming, the crew of a ship about to weigh anchor, a procession, an angry mob, — these have something about them that is epic and sublime; so any peasant, if we see in him an epitome of race or class, with his historic consequence and his unconscious majesty, may and ought to interest us. The *payo* of Avila who passes me indifferently in the street; the beggar in Burgos who asks an alms with courteous dignity, wrapped in his tattered clothes as though they were garments of costly cloth; the Gallician lad who guides his yoke of oxen and creaking cart, — these not only stir in my soul a sentiment of patriotism, but they have for me an æsthetic charm which I never feel in the presence of a dress-coat and a stiff hat. Perhaps this effect depends rather on the spectator, and it may be our fancy that produces it; for, as regards the Russian peasant, those who know him well say that he is by nature practical and positive, and not at all inclined to the romantic and sentimental. The Sclav race is a rich poetic wellspring, but it depends upon what one means by poetry. For example, in love matters, the Russian peasant is docile and prosaic to the last degree. The hardy rustic is supposed to need two indispensable accessories for his work, — a woman and a horse; the latter is procured for him by the head or *old man* of the house, the former by the *old woman;* the wedding is nothing more than the matriculation of the farmer; the pair is incorporated with the great family, the agricultural commune, and that is the end of the idyl. Amorous and gallant conduct among peasants would be little fitting, given the low estimation in which women are held. Although the Russian peasant considers the woman independent, subject neither to father nor husband, invested with equal rights with men; and although the widow or the unmarried woman who is head of the house takes part in the deliberations of the *mir* and may even exercise in it the powers of a mayor (and in order to preserve this independence many peasant-women remain unmarried), this consideration is purely a social one, and individually the woman has no rights whatever. A song of the people says that seven women together have not so much as one soul, rather none at all, for their soul is smoke. The theory of marriage relations is that the husband ought to love his wife as he does his own soul, to measure and treasure her as he does his sheepskin coat: the rod sanctions the contract. In some provinces of Finnish or Tartar origin the bride is still bought and sold like a head of cattle; it is sometimes the custom still to steal her, or to feign a rape, symbolizing indeed the idea of woman as a slave and the booty of war. So rigorous is the matrimonial yoke, that parricides are numerous, and the jury, allowing attenuating circumstances, generally pardons them.

Tikomirov, who, though a radical, is a wise and sensible man, says, that far from considering the masses of the people as models worthy of imitation, he finds them steeped in absolute ignorance, the victims of every abuse and of administrative immorality; deprived for many centuries of intercourse with civilized nations, they have not outgrown the infantile period, they are superstitious, idolatrous, and pagan, as shown by their legends and popular songs. They believe blindly in witchcraft, to the extent that to discredit a political party with them one has only to insinuate that it is given to the use of sorcery and the black arts. The peasant has also an unconquerable propensity to stealing, lying, servility, and drunkenness. Wherefore, then, is he judged superior to the other classes of society?

In spite of the puerile humility to which the Russian peasant is predisposed by long years of subjection, he yet obeys a democratic impulse toward equality, which servitude has not obliterated; the Russian does not understand the English peasant's respect for the *gentleman*, nor the French reverence for the *chevalier* well-dressed and decorated. When the government of Poland ordered certain Cossack executions of the nobility, these children of the steppes asked one another, " Brother, has the shadow of my body increased?" Taught to govern himself, thanks to the municipal regimen, the Russian peasant manifests in a high degree the sentiment of human equality, an idea both Christian and democratic, rather more deeply rooted in those countries governed by absolute monarchy and municipal liberty, than in those of parliamentary institutions. The Spaniard says, " None lower than the King;" the Russian says the same with respect to the Czar. Primitive and credulous, a philosopher in his way, the dweller on the Russian steppes wields a dynamic force displayed in history by collectivities, be the moral value of the individual what it may. In nations like Russia, in which the upper classes are educated abroad, and are, like water, reflectors and nothing more, the originality, the poetry, the epic element, is always with the masses of the people, which comes out strong and beautiful in supreme moments, a faithful custodian of the national life, as for example when the butcher Minine saved his country from the yoke of Sweden, or when, before the French invasion of 1812, they organized bands of guerillas, or set fire to Moscow.

Hence in Russia, as in France prior to the Revolution, many thinkers endeavor to revive the antiquated theory of the Genevan philosopher, and proclaim the superiority of the natural man, by contact with whom society, infected with Occidental senility, must be regenerated. Discouraged by the incompatibility between the imported European progress and the national tradition, unable to still the political strife of a country where pessimist solutions are most natural and weighty, their patriotism now uplifts, now shatters their hopes, even in the case of those who disclaim and condemn individual patriotism, such as Count Tolstoï; and then ensues the apotheosis of the past, the veneration of national heroes and of the people. "The people is great," says Turguenief in his novel "Smoke;" "we are mere ragamuffins." And so *the people*, which still bears traces of the marks of servitude, has been converted into a mysterious divinity, the inspiration of enthusiastic canticles.

VII.

SOCIAL CLASSES IN RUSSIA.

PROPERLY speaking, there are no social classes in Russia, a phenomenon which èxplains to some extent the political life and internal constitution; there is no co-ordinate proportion between the rural and the urban element, and at first sight one sees in this vast empire only the innumerable mass of peasants, just as on the map one sees only a wide and monotonous plain. Although it is true that a rural and commercial aristocracy did arise and flourish in old Moscow in the twelfth and thirteenth centuries, the era of invasions, yet the passions of the wars that followed gave it the death-blow. The middle classes in the rich and independent republics lost their wealth and influence, and the people, being unable of themselves to reorganize the State, sustained the princes, who soon became autocrats, ready at the first chance to subdue the nobles and unite the disintegrated and war-worn nation. With the subdivision into independent principalities and the institution of democratic municipalities the importance of the cities decreased, and the privileged classes were at an end. The middle class is the least important. In the same districts where formerly it was most powerful it has been dissolved by the continuous infusion of the peasant element, owing to the curious custom of emigration, which is spontaneous with this nomadic and colonizing people. Many farmers, although enrolled in the rural villages, spend a large part of the year in the city, filling some office, and forming a hybrid class between the rural and artisan classes, thus sterilizing the natural instincts of the laboring proletariat by the enervation of city life. The emperors were not blind to the disproportion between the civic and rural elements, and have endeavored to remedy it. The industrial and commercial population fled from the cities to escape the taxes; therefore they promulgated laws prohibiting emigration and the renunciation of civic rights, under severe penalties. Yet with all these the cities have taken but a second place in Russian history. Western annals are full of sieges, defences, and mutinies of cities; in Russia we hear only of the insurrection of wandering tribes or hordes of peasants. Russian cities exist and live only at the mandate or protection of the emperor. Every one knows what extraordinary means were taken by Peter the Great to build St. Petersburg upon the swamps along the Neva; in twenty-three years that remarkable woman called the Semiramis of the North founded no less than two hundred and sixteen cities, determined to create a mesocratic element, to the lack of which she attributed the ignorance and misery of her empire. Whenever we see any rapid advancement in Russia we may be sure it is the work of autocracy, a beneficence of despotism (that word so shocking to our ears). It was despotism which created the modern capital opposite the old Byzantine, legendary, retrogressive town, — the new so different from the old, so full of the revolutionary spirit, its streets undermined by conspirators, its pavements red with the blood of a murdered Czar. These cities, colleges, schools, universities, theatres, founded by imperial and autocratic hands, were the cradle of the political unrest that rebels against their power ; were there no cities, there would be no revolutions in Russia. Although they do not harbor crowds of famishing authors like those of London and Paris, who lie in wait for the day of sack and ruin, yet they are full of a strange element composed of people of divers extraction and condition, and of small intellect, but who call themselves emphatically *the intelligence of Russia.*

I have felt compelled to render justice to the good will of the autocrats ; and to be equally just I must say that whatever has advanced culture in Russia has proceeded from the nobility, and this without detriment to the fact that the larger energies lie with the masses of the people. The enlightenment and thirst for progress manifested by the nobility is everywhere apparent in Russian history. They are descended from the retinues of the early Muscovite Czars, to whom were given wealth and lands on condition of military service, and they are therefore in their origin unlike any other European nobility ; they have known nothing of feudalism, nor the Germanic symbolism of blazons, arms, titles, and privileges, pride of race and notions of caste : these have had no influence over them. The Boyars, who are the remnants of the ancient territorial aristocracy, on losing their sovereign rights, rallied round the Czar in the quality of court councillors, and received gold and treasure in abundance, but never the social importance of the Spanish grandee or the French baron. Hence the Russian aristocracy was an instrument of power, but without class interests, replenished continually by the infusion of elements from other social classes, for no barrier prevented the peasant from becoming a merchant and the merchant from becoming a noble, if the fates were kind There are legally two classes of aristocracy in Russia, — the transmissible, or hereditary, and the personal, which is not hereditary. If the latter surprise us for a moment, it soon strikes us with favor, since we all acknowledge to an occasional or frequent protest against the idea of hereditary nobility, as when we lament that men of glorious renown are represented by unworthy or insignificant descendants. In Russia, Krilof, the Æsop of Moscow, as he is called, put this protest into words in the fable of the peasant who was leading a flock of geese to the city to sell. The geese complained of the unkindness with which they were treated, adding that they were entitled to respect as being the descendants of the famous birds that saved the Capitol, and to whom Rome had dedicated a feast. "And what great thing have *you* done?" asked the peasant. "We? Oh, nothing." "Then to the oven!" he replied.

The only title of purely national origin in Russia

is that of prince;[1] all others are of recent importation from Europe; in the family of the prince, as in that of the humblest *mujik*, the sons are equals in rights and honors, and the fortune of the father, as well as his title, descends equally to all. Feudalism, the basis of nobility as a class, never existed in Russia: according to Sclavophiles, because Russia never suffered conquest in those ancient times; according to positivist historians, by reason of geographical structure which did not favor seignorial castles and bounded domains, or any other of those appurtenances of feudalism dear to romance and poetry, and really necessary to its existence, — the moated wall, the mole overhanging some rocky precipice washed by an angry torrent, and below at its foot, like a hen-roost beneath a vulture's nest, the clustered huts of the vassals. But we have seen that the Russian nobility acknowledges no law of superiority; like the people, they hold the idea of divisible and common property. Hence this aristocracy, less haughty than that of Europe, ruled by imperial power, subject until the time of Peter III. to insulting punishment by whip or rod, and which, at the caprice of the Czar, might at any time be degraded

---

[1] "The term translated 'prince' perhaps needs some explanation. A Russian prince may be a bootblack or a ferryman. The word *kniaz* denotes a descendant of any of the hundreds of petty rulers, who before the time of the unification of Russia held the land. They all claim descent from the semi-mythical Rurik; and as every son of a *kniaz* bears the title, it may be easily imagined how numerous they are. The term 'prince,' therefore, is really a too high-sounding title to represent it." — NATHAN HASKELL DOLE.

to the quality of buffoons for any neglect of a code of honor imposed by the traditions of their race, — never drew apart from the life of the nation, and, on the contrary, was always foremost in intellectual matters. Russian literature proves this, for it is the work of the Russian nobility mainly, and the ardent sympathy for the people displayed in it is another confirmation. Tolstoï, a noble, feels an irrepressible tenderness, a physical attraction toward the peasant; Turguenief, a noble and a rich man, in his early years consecrated himself by a sort of vow to the abolition of servitude.

The same lack of class prejudices has made the Russian nobility a quick soil for the repeated ingrafting of foreign culture according to the fancy of the emperors. Catherine II. found little difficulty in modelling her court after that of Versailles; but the same aristocracy that powdered and perfumed itself at her behest adopted more important reforms to a degree that caused Count Rostopchine to exclaim, " I can understand the French citizen's lending a hand in the revolution to acquire his rights, but I cannot understand the Russian's doing the same to lose his." They are so accustomed to holding the first place in intellectual matters, that no privilege seems comparable to that of standing in the vanguard of advanced thought. They had been urged to frequent the lyceums and debating societies, to take up serious studies and scientific education by the word of rulers who were enlightened, and friends to progress (as were many of them), when all at once sciences and studies, books and the press, began to be suspected, the censorship was established, and the conspiracy of December was the signal for the rupture between authority and the liberal thought of the country. But the nobles who had tasted òf the fruit of the knowledge of good and evil did not resign themselves easily to the limited horizon offered by the School of Pages or the antechamber of the palace ; their hand was upon the helm, and rather than let it go they generously immolated their material interests and social importance. The aristocracy is everywhere else the support of the throne, but in Russia it is a destroying element; and while the people remains attached to the autocrat, the nobles learn in the very schools founded by the emperors to pass judgment upon the supreme authority and to criticise the sovereign. Nicholas I. did not fail to realize that these establishments of learning were focuses of revolutionary ardor, and he systematically reduced the number of students and put limits to scientific education.

It follows that the most reactionary class, or the most unstable class in Russia, the class painted in darkest colors by the novelists and used as a target for their shafts by the satirists, is not the noble but the bureaucratic, the office-holders, the members of the *tchin* (an institution Asiatic in form, comparable perhaps to a Chinese mandarinate). Peter the Great, in his zeal to set everything in order, drew up the famous categories wherein the Russian official microcosm is divided into a double series of fourteen

grades each, from ecclesiastical dignitaries to the
military. This Asiatic sort of machinery (though
conceived by the great imitator of the West) became
generally abhorred, and excited a national antipathy,
less perhaps for its hollow formalism than on account
of the proverbial immorality of the officers catalogued
in it. Mercenariness, pride, routine, and indolence
are the capital sins of the Russian office-holder, and
the first has so strong a hold upon him that the
people say, "To make yourself understood by him
you must talk of rubles;" adding that in Russia
everybody robs but Christ, who cannot because his
hands are nailed down. Corruption is general; it
mounts upward like a turbid wave from the humblest
clerk to the archduke, generalissimo, or admiral.
It is a tremendous ulcer, that can only be cured
by a cautery of literary satire, the avenging muse of
Gogol, and the dictatorial initiative of the Czars. In
a country governed by parliamentary institutions it
would be still more difficult to apply a remedy.

The contrast is notable between the odium inspired
by the bureaucracy and the sympathy that greets the
municipal institutions, — not only those of a patriarchal
character such as the *mir*, but those too of a more
modern origin. Among the latter may be mentioned
the *zemstvo*, or territorial assembly, analogous to our
provincial deputations, but of more liberal stripe,
and entirely decentralized. In this all classes are
represented, and not, as in the *mir*, the peasants
merely. The form of this local parliament is extremely
democratic; the cities, the peasants, and the

property-holders elect separate representatives, and the assembly devotes itself to the consideration of plain but interesting practical questions of hygiene, salubrity, safety, and public instruction. This offers another opportunity to the nobility, for this body engages itself particularly with the well-being and progress of the poorer classes, in providing physicians for the villages in place of the ignorant herb-doctors, in having the *mujiks* taught to read, and in guarding their poor wooden houses from fire.

While the Russian nobility has never slept, the Russian clergy, on the contrary, has been permanently wrapped in lethargy. The rôle accorded to the Greek Church is dull and depressing, a petrified image, fixed and archaic as the *icons*, or sacred pictures, which still copy the coloring and design of the Byzantine epoch. Ever since it was rent by schism from the parent trunk of Catholicism, life has died in its roots and the sap has frozen in its veins. Since Peter the Great abolished the Patriarchy, the ecclesiastical authority resides in a Synod composed of prelates elected by the government. According to the ecclesiastical statutes, the emperor is Head of the church, supreme spiritual chief; and though there has been promulgated no dogma of his infallibility, it amounts to the same in effect, for he may bind and loose at will. At the Czar's command the church anathematizes, as when for example to-day the *popes* are ordered to preach against the growing desire for partition of land, against socialism, and against the political enemies of the government; the priest is given a model sermon after which he must pattern his own; and such is his humiliation that sometimes he is obliged by order of the Synod to send information, obtained through his office as confessor, to the police, thus revealing the secrets of confiding souls. What a loss of self-respect must follow such a proceeding! Is it a marvel that some independent schismatics called *raskolniks*, revivalists and followers of ancient rites and truths, should thrive upon the decadence of the official clergy, who are subjected to such insulting servitude and must give to Cæsar what belongs to God?

In view of these facts it is in vain to boast of spiritual independence and say that the Greek church knows no head but Christ. The government makes use of the clergy as of one arm more, which, however, is now almost powerless through corruption. The Oriental church has no conception of the noble devotion which has honored Catholicism in the lives of Saint Thomas of Canterbury and Cardinal Cisneros.

The Russian clergy is divided into *black* and *white*, or regular and secular; the former, powerful and rich, rule in ecclesiastical administration; the latter vegetate in the small villages, ill paid and needy, using their wits to live at the expense of their parishioners, and to wheedle them out of a dozen eggs or a handful of meal. Is it strange that the parishioner respects them but little? Is it strange that the *pope* lives in gross pride or scandalous immorality, and that we read of his stealing money from under the pillow of a dying man, of one who baptized a dog, of another who was ducked in a frozen pond by his *barino*, or landlord, for the amusement of his guests? It is true that a few occasional facts prove nothing against a class, and that malice will produce from any source hurtful anecdotes and more or less profane details touching sacred things; but to my mind, that which tells most strongly against the Russian clergy is its inanity, its early intellectual death, which shut it out completely from scientific reflection, controversy, and apology, and therefore from all philosophy, — realms in which the Catholic clergy has excelled. Like a stripped and lifeless trunk the Oriental church produces no theologians, thinkers, or *savants*. There are none to elaborate, define, and ramify her dogmas; the human mind in her sounds no depths of mystery. If there are no conflicts between religion and science in Russia, it is because the Muscovite church weighs not a shadow with the free-thinkers.

Certainly the adherents and members of the earlier church bear away the palm for culture and spiritual independence. At the close of the seventeenth century, after the struggles with Sweden and Poland, the schismatic church aroused the national conscience, and satisfied, to a certain extent, the moral needs of a race naturally religious by temperament. It began to discuss liturgical minutiæ, and persecuted delinquents so fiercely that it infused all dissenters with a spirit of protest against an authority which was disposed to treat them like bandits or wild beasts. Such persecution demonstrates the fact that not only ecclesiastical but secular power is irritated by heterodoxy. In Russia, whose slumbering church is unmoved even by a thunder-bolt, an instinct of orderliness led the less devout of the emperors against the schismatics. To-day there are from twelve to fifteen millions of schismatics and sects; and many among them are given to the coarsest superstitions, practise obscene and cruel rites, worship the Devil, and mutilate themselves in their insane fervors. Probably Russia is the only country in the civilized world to-day where superstition, quietism, and mysticism, without law or limit, grow like poisonous trees; and in my work on Saint Francis of Assisi I have remarked how the communist heresies of the Middle Ages have survived there in the North. Some authors affirm that the clergy shut their eyes and open their hands to receive hush-money for their tolerance of heterodoxy. But let us not be too ready always to believe the worst. Only lately there fell into my hands an article written by that much respected author, Melchior de Voguié, who assures us that he has observed signs of regeneration in many Russian parishes.

From this review of social classes in Russia it may be deduced that the peasant masses are the repository of national energies, while the nobility has until now displayed the most apparent activity. The proof of this is to be found in the consideration of a memorable historical event, — the greatest perhaps that the present century has known, — the emancipation of the serfs.

VIII.

RUSSIAN SERFDOM.

Russia boasts of never having known that black stain upon ancient civilizations, slavery; but the pretension, notwithstanding many allegations thereto in her own chronicles, is refuted by Herodotus, who speaks of the inhuman treatment inflicted by the Scythians on their slaves, even putting out their eyes that they might better perform certain tasks; and the same historian refers to the treachery of the slaves to their masters in raping the women while they were at war with the Medes, and to the insurrection of these slaves which was put down by the Scythians by means of the whip alone, — the whip being in truth a characteristic weapon of a country accustomed to servitude. Herodotus does say in another place that "among the Scythians the king's servants are free youths well-born, for it is not the custom in Scythia to buy slaves;" from which it may be inferred that the slaves were prisoners of war. Howbeit, Russian authors insist that in their country serfs were never slaves, and serfdom was rather an abuse of the power of the nobility and the government than an historic natural result.

To my mind this is not so; and I must say that I think servitude had an actual beginning, and that there was a cause for it. The Muscovite empire was but sparsely populated, and the population was by temperament adventurous, nomadic, restless, and expansive. We have observed that the limitless plains of Russia offer no climatic antagonisms, for the reason that there are no climatic boundaries; but it was not merely the love of native province that was lacking in the Russian, but the attachment to the paternal roof and to the home village. It is said that the origin of this sentiment is embedded in rock; where dwellings are built of wood and burn every seven years on an average, there is no such thing as the paternal roof, there is no such thing as home. With his hatchet in his belt the Russian peasant will build another house wherever a new horizon allures him. But if the scanty rural population scatters itself over the steppes, it will be lost in it as the sand drinks in the rain, and the earth will remain unploughed and waste; there will be nothing to tax, and nobody to do military service. Therefore, about the end of the sixteenth century, when all the rest of Europe was beginning to feel the stirrings of political liberty and the breath of the Renaissance, the Regent, Boris Godonof, riveted the chains of slavery upon the wrists of many millions of human beings in Russia. It is very true that Russian servitude does not mean the subjection of man to man, but to the soil; for the decree of Godonof converted the peasant into a slave merely by abrogating the traditional right of the "black man" to change his living-place on Saint George's day. The peasant perceived no other change in his condition than that of finding himself fastened, chained, bound to the soil. The Russian word which we translate "serf" means "consolidated," "adherent."

It is easy to see the historical transition from the free state to that of servitude. The military and political organization of the Russian State in the twelfth and thirteenth centuries hedged in the peasant's liberty of action, and his situation began to resemble that of the Roman *colonus*, or husbandman, who was neither "bond nor free." When the nation was constituted upon firmer bases, it seemed indispensable to fix every man's limitation, to range the population in classes, and to lay upon them obligations consistent with the needs of the empire. These bonds were imposed just as the other peoples of Europe were breaking away from theirs.

Servitude, or serfdom, did not succeed throughout the empire, however. Siberia and the independent Cossacks of the South rejected it; only passive consent could sanction a condition that was not the fruit of conquest nor had as an excuse the right of the strongest. Even in the rest of Russia the peasant never was entirely submissive, never willingly bent his neck to the yoke, and the seventeenth and eighteenth centuries witnessed bitter and sanguinary uprisings of the serfs, who were prompt to follow the first impostor who pronounced words of promise; and, strange to say, what was most galling was his entail upon the land rather than the deprivation of his own liberty. He imagined that the lord of the whole earth was the Czar, that by his favor it was temporarily in possession of the nobles, but that in truth and justice it belonged to him who tilled it. Pugatchef, the pretender to the title of Peter III., in order to rally to his standard an innumerable host of peasants, called himself the rural emperor, and declared that no sooner should he gain the throne of his ancestors than he would shower treasure upon the nobles and restore the land to the tillers of it.

Those who forged the fetters of serfdom had little faith in the stability of it, however. And although the abuses arising out of it were screened and tacitly consented to, — and never more so than during the reign of the humane philosopher, friend, and correspondent of Voltaire, the Empress Catherine II., — yet law and custom forever refused to sanction them. Russian serfdom assumed rather a patriarchal character, and this softened its harshness. It was considered iniquitous to alienate the serfs, and it was only lawful in case of parting with the land whereon those serfs labored; in this way was preserved the thin line of demarcation between agrarian servitude and slavery.

There were, however, serfs in worse condition, true helots, namely, the domestic servants, who were at the mercy of the master's caprice, like the fowls in his poultry-yard. Each proprietor maintained a numerous household below stairs, useless and idle as a rule, whose children he brought up and had instructed in certain ways in order to hire them out or sell them by and by. The players in the theatres were generally recruited from this class, and until

Alexander I. prohibited such shameless traffic, it was not uncommon to see announced in the papers the sale of a coachman beside that of a Holstein cow. But like every other institution which violates and offends human conscience, Russian serfdom could not exist forever, in spite of some political and social advantages to the empire.

Certain Russian writers affirm that the assassination of masters and proprietors was of frequent occurrence in the days of serfdom, and that even now the peasant is disposed to quarrels and acts of violence against the nobles. Yet, on the whole, I gather from my reading on the subject that the relations in general between the serf and the master were, on the one side, humble, reverent, and filial; on the other, kind, gentle, and protecting. The important question for the peasant is that of the practical ownership of the land. It is not his freedom but his agrarian rights that have been restored to him; and this must be borne in mind in order to understand why the recent emancipation has not succeeded in pacifying the public mind and bringing about a new and happy Russia.

Given the same problem to the peasant and the man of mind, it will be safe to say that they will solve it in very different ways, if not in ways diametrically opposed. The peasant will be guided by the positive and concrete aspect of the matter; the man of mind by the speculative and ideal. The peasant calculates the influence of atmospheric phenomena upon his crops, while the other observes the beauty of the sunset or the tranquillity of the night. In social questions the peasant demands immediate utility, no matter how small it may be, while the other demands the application of principles and the triumph of ideas. Under the care of a master the Russian serf enjoyed a certain material welfare, and if he fell to the lot of a good master — and Russian masters have the reputation of being in general excellent — his situation was not only tolerable but advantageous. On the other hand, the intelligent could not put up with the monstrous and iniquitous fact of human liberty being submitted to the arbitrary rule of a master who could apply the lash at will, sell men like cattle, and dispose as he would of bodies and souls. Where this exists, since Christ came into the world, either there is no knowledge, or the ignominy must be stamped out.

We all know that celebrated story of "Uncle Tom's Cabin," the famous Abolitionist novel by Mrs. Harriet Beecher Stowe. There were also novelists in Russia who set themselves to plead for the emancipation of the serfs. But there is a difference between them and the North American authoress, in that the Russians, in order to achieve their object, had no need to exaggerate the reality, to paint sensitive slaves and children that die of pity, but, with an artistic instinct, they appealed to æsthetic truth to obtain human justice. "Dead Souls," by Gogol, or one of the poetical and earnest *brochures* of Turguenief, awakens a more stirring and permanent indignation than the sentimental allegory of Mrs. Stowe; and neither Gogol nor Turguenief misrepresented the serf or defamed the master, but rather they present to us both as they were in life, scorning recourse to bad taste for the sake of capturing tender hearts. The noblest sentiments of the soul, divine compassion, equity, righteous vengeance, the generous pity that moves to sacrifice, rise to the inspired voice of great writers; we see the abuse, we feel it, it hurts us, it oppresses us, and by a spontaneous impulse we desire the good and abhor the evil. This enviable privilege has been granted to the Russian novelists; had they no greater glory, this would suffice to save them from oblivion.

The Abolitionist propaganda subtly and surely spread through the intelligent classes, created an opinion, communicated itself naturally to the press in as far as the censor permitted, and little by little the murmur grew in volume, like that raised against the administrative corruption after the Crimean War. And it is but just to add that the Czars were never behind in this national movement. Had it not been for their omnipotent initiative, who knows if even now slavery would not stain the face of Europe? There is reason to believe it when one sees the obstacles that hinder other reforms in Russia in which the autocrat takes no part. Doubtless the mind of the emperor was influenced by the words of Alexander II., in 1856, to the Muscovite nobles: "It is better to abolish serfdom by decrees from above than to wait for it to be destroyed by an impulse from below." A purely human motive; yet in every generous act there may be a little egotistical leaven. Let us not judge the unfortunate Emancipator too severely.

The Crimean War and its grave internal consequences aided to undermine the infamous institution of serfdom, at the same time that it disclosed the hidden cancer of the administration, the misgovernment and ruin of the nation. With the ill success of the campaign, Russia clearly saw the need for self-examination and reorganization. Among the many and pressing questions presented to her, the most urgent was that of the serfs, and the impossibility of re-forming a prosperous State, modern and healthy, while this taint existed within her. Alexander II., whose variability and weakness are no bar to his claim of the honored title of the Liberator, exhorted the aristocracy to consummate this great work, and (a self-abnegation worthy of all praise, and which only a blind political passion can deny them) the nobles coincided and co-operated with him with perfect good faith, and even with the electrical enthusiasm characteristic of the Sclavic race. One cannot cease to extol this noble act, which, taken as a whole, is sublime, although, being the work of large numbers, it may be overloaded with details and incidents in which the interest flags. It may be easy to preach a reform whose aims do not hurt our pride, shatter our fortunes, alter our way of living, or conflict with the ideas inculcated upon us in childhood by our parents; but to do this to one's own detriment deserves especial recognition. The nobility on this occasion only put into practice certain theories which had stirred in their hearts of old. The first great Russian poet, Prince Kantemire, wrote in 1738, in his satires, that Adam did not beget nobles, nor did Noah save in the ark any but his equals, — humble husbandmen, famous only for their virtues. To my mind the best praise to the Russian nobility is for having offered less hindrance to the emancipation of the serfs than the North American democracy to the liberation of the slaves; and I solicit especial applause for this self-sacrificing, redeeming aristocracy.

The fruits of the emancipation were not what desire promised. The peasants, from their positivist point of view, set little value on liberty itself, and scarcely understood it. "We are yours," they were accustomed to say to their masters; "but the soil is ours." When it became known that they must go on paying even for the goods of the community, they rebelled; they declared that emancipation was a farce, a lie, and that true emancipation ought to abolish rent and distribute the land in equal parts. Did not the proclamation of the Czar read that they were free? Well, freedom, in their language, meant emancipation from labor, and the possession of the land. One *mir* even sent a deputation to the governor, announcing that as he had been a good master he would still be allowed the use and profit of his house and farm. The peasant believed himself free from all obligation, and even refused to work until the government forced him to do so; and the result was that the lash and the rod were never so frequently laid across Russian shoulders as in the first three years of emancipation and liberty.

What cared they — "the little black men" — for the dignity of the freeman or the rights of citizenship? That which laid strongest hold of their primitive imagination was the desire to possess the whole land, — the old dream of what they called the *black partition*, the national Utopia. One Russian revolutionary journal adopted the name of "Land and Liberty," a magic motto to a peasant country, giving the former the first place, or at least making the two synonymous. The Russian people ask no political rights, but rather the land which is watered by the sweat of their brow; and if some day the anarchists — the agitators who go from village to village propagating their sanguinary doctrines — succeed in awakening and stirring this Colossus to action, it will be by touching this tender spot and alluring by the promise of this traditional dream. The old serf lives in hopes of a Messiah, be he emperor or conspirator, who shall deliver the earth into his hands; and at times the vehemence of this insatiable desire brings forth popular prophets, who announce that the millennium is at hand, and that by the will of Heaven the land is to be divided among the cultivators thereof. From his great love to the autocrat the peasant believes that *he* also desires this distribution, but being hampered by his counsellors and menaced by his courtiers, he cannot authorize it yet. "For," says the peasant, "the land never belonged to the lords, but first to the sovereign and then to the *mir*." The idea of individual proprietorship is so repugnant to this people that they say that even death is beautiful shared in common.

All the schismatic sects in Russia preach community of possessions. Some among them live better than the orthodox Greeks; some are voluntarily consecrated to absolute poverty, such as characterized the early orders of mendicants, and literally give their cloak to him who asks; but both the more temperate and the fanatics agree in the faith of the general and indisputable right of man to possess the land he cultivates.

With society as with the individual, after great effort comes prostration, after a sudden change, inevitable uneasiness. So with Russian emancipation. Although in some localities the condition of the peasants was ameliorated, in others their misery and retrogression seemed only to increase, and led them to pine for the old bonds. The abuse, arbitrariness, and cruelty which are cited, and which shock the nerves of Westerners, caused no alarm to the Russian peasant, who was well used to baring his back in payment for any delinquency. The worst extent to which the master allowed his anger to spend itself was an unlimited number of stripes; and this very punishment, which to-day no master would inflict, and which the law expressly forbids, is still frequently imposed by the peasant tribunals of the *volost* or canton; their confidence in its efficacy is well grounded, and it is well authorized by custom and experience. What the peasant fears and hates most is not the rod or the whip, but the rent-collector, the tax-gatherer, the burden of the taxes themselves, and hunger.

What must be the æsthetic and political determination of this race, which prefers the possession of the soil to the liberty of the individual? In literature, toward a plain and candid realism; in form of government, a communist absolutism. The abstract constitutional idea, which, in spite of its Anglo-Saxon origin, meets perfectly the ideal entertained by Latin minds, has no charm for the Sclav. Yet at the same time the Russian combines, with his practical and concrete notions of life and his preponderating sense of realism, a dreamy and childlike imagination, which acts upon him like a dangerous dose of opium.

In the next essay I propose to show how there has grown up within this patient and submissive rural people, and has finally burst forth, that most terrible of revolutionary volcanoes, nihilism.

Book II.

RUSSIAN NIHILISM AND ITS LITERATURE.

I.

THE WORD "NIHILISM."

I HAVE scarcely realized until now the difficulties in the way of the subject I am treating. To talk of nihilism is an audacious undertaking, and in spite of all my endeavors to hold the balance true, and to consider calmly the social phenomena and the literature into which it has infiltrated, I shall perhaps not be able to avoid a note of partiality or emotion. To some I shall seem too indulgent with the Russian revolutionaries, and they may say of me, as of M. Leroy-Beaulieu, that my opinions are imbibed from official sources and my words taken from the mouth of reactionaries.

The first stumbling-block is the word "nihilism." In Tikomirov's work on Russia seven or eight pages are devoted to the severe condemnation of the use of the expressions "nihilism" and "nihilist." Nevertheless, at the risk of offending my friend the author, I must make use of them, since, as he himself allows, they are employed universally, and all the world understands what is meant by them in an approximate and relative way. I do not reject the term proposed by Tikomirov, who would call nihilism "the militant intelligence;" but this is much too long and obscure, and before accepting it, it behooves one to understand what is meant by *Russian intelligence*. The nihilists call themselves by a variety of names, — democrats, socialists, propagandists, *new men*, or sometimes by the title of some organ of their clandestine press. This war of names seems puerile, and I prefer to face the fury of Tikomirov against those who not only use the objectionable term but dedicate a chapter to what it represents, and study nihilism as a doctrine or tendency distinct among all that have arisen until now. I cannot agree to the idea that nihilism is merely a Russian intellectual movement, nor do I think that all Europe is mistaken in judging that the nihilist explosions are characteristic of the great Sclav empire. On the contrary, I believe that if Russia were to-morrow blotted from the map, and her history and every trace of her national individuality obliterated, only a few pages of her romances and a few fragments of her revolutionary literature being left to us, a philosopher or a critic could reconstruct, without other data, the spirit of the race in all its integrity and completeness.

Now, to begin, how did this much-discussed word originate? It was a novelist who first baptized the party who called themselves at that time *new men*.

It was Ivan Turguenief, who by the mouth of one of the characters in his celebrated novel, "Fathers and Sons," gave the young generation the name of nihilists. But it was not of his coinage; Royer-Collard first stamped it; Victor Hugo had already said that the negation of the infinite led directly to nihilism, and Joseph Lemaistre had spoken of the nihilism, more or less sincere, of the contemporary generations; but it was reserved for the author of "Virgin Soil" to bring to light and make famous this word, which after making a great stir in his own country attracted the attention of the whole world.

The reign of Nicholas I. was an epoch of hard oppression. When he ascended the throne, the conspiracy of the Decembrists broke out, and this sudden revelation of the revolutionary spirit steeled the already inflexible soul of the Czar. Nicholas, although fond of letters and an assiduous reader of Homer, was disposed to throttle his enemies, and would not have hesitated to pluck out the brains of Russia; he was very near suppressing all the universities and schools, and inaugurating a voluntary retrocession to Asiatic barbarism. He did mutilate and reduce the instruction, he suppressed the chair of European political laws, and after the events of 1848 in France he seriously considered the idea of closing his frontiers with a cordon of troops to beat back foreign liberalism like the cholera or the plague. Those who have had a near view of this Iron Czar have described him to me as tall, straight, stiff, always in uniform, a slave to his duties as sovereign, the living personification of the autocrat, and called, not without reason, the Quixote of absolutism. At the close of a life devoted to the fanatical inculcation of his convictions, this inflexible emperor, who believed himself to be guided by the Divine hand, saw only the dilapidation and ruin of his country, which then started up dismayed and raised a cry of reprobation, a chorus of malediction against the emperor and the order of things established by him. Satire cried out in strident and indignant tones, and spit in the face of the Czar with terrible anathemas. "Oh, Emperor," it said to him, "Russia confided the supreme power to you; you were as a god upon the earth. What have you done? Blinded by ignorance and selfishness, you longed for power and forgot Russia; you spent your life in reviewing troops, in changing uniforms, in signing decrees. You created the vile race of press-censors, so that you might sleep in peace, that you might ignore the needs of the people, and turn a deaf ear to their cries; and the truth you buried deep, and rolled a great stone over the door of the sepulchre, and put a guard over it, so that you might think in your proud heart that it would never rise again. But the light of the third day is breaking, and truth will come forth from among the dead." And so the great autocrat heard the crash of the walls that he had built with callous hands and cemented with the blood and tears of two millions of human beings whom he had exiled to Siberia. Perhaps the inflexible principles, the mainspring of his hard soul, gave way then; but it was indeed too late to give the lie to his whole life, and according to well-authenticated reports he sought a sure and speedy death by wilful exposure to the rigors of the terrible climate. "I cannot go back," were the dying words of this upright and consistent man, who, notwithstanding his hardness, was yet not a tyrant.

However, it was under his sceptre, under his systematic suppression, that, by confession of the great revolutionary statesman Herzen, Russian thought developed as never before; that the emancipation of the intelligence, which this very statesman calls a tragic event, was accomplished, and a national literature was brought to light and began to flourish. When Alexander II. succeeded to the throne, when the bonds of despotism were loosened and the blockade with which Nicholas vainly tried to isolate his empire was raised, the field was ready for the intellectual and political strife.

Russia is prone to violent extremes in everything. No social changes are brought about in her with the slow gradations which make transitions easy and avoid shocks and collisions. In the rest of Europe modern scientific progress was due to numerous coincident causes, such as the Renaissance, the art of printing, the discovery of America; but in Russia the will of the autocrat was the motor, and the country was forced and surprised into it. And when this drowsy land one day shakes off its lethargy and takes note of the latent political effervescence within itself, it will be with the same fiery earnestness, the same exaggeration, the same logical directness, straight to the end, even though that end culminate in absurdity.

Before explaining how nihilism is the outcome of intelligence, we must understand what is meant by intelligence in Russia. It means a class composed of all those, of whatever profession or estate, who have at heart the advancement of intellectual life, and contribute in every way toward it. It may be said, indeed, that such a class is to be found in every country; but there is this difference, — in other countries the class is not a unit; there are factions, or a large number of its members shun political and social discussion in order to enjoy the serene atmosphere of the world of art, while in Russia *the intelligence* means a common cause, a homogeneous spirit, subversive and revolutionary withal. To write a history of modern literature, particularly of the novel, in Russia, is equivalent to writing the history of the revolution.

The subversive, dissolvent character of this intelligence — working now tacitly, now openly, and with a candor surprising in a country subjected to such suspicious censorship — explains why the czars, once the protectors of the arts, have become since the middle of this century so out of humor with authors, books, and the press. We have heard of one emperor — the cleverest of them all — who in the interest of his reforms had his own son whipped to death. Russian art, also son of the czars, figuratively speaking, received scarcely better treatment when it signified a desire to stand on its own feet.

Long and painful is the list of persecutions directed

against the growth of Thought, in prose and verse, and above all against illustrious men. But we must make a distinction, so as not to be unjust. Herzen, exiled and deprived of all his possessions, and the famous martyr Tchernichewsky, confined twenty and odd years in a Siberian prison or fortress, do not arouse our astonishment, for they suffered the common fate of the political agitator; but it seems a pity that such artists as Dostoiëwsky and Turguenief should suffer any such infliction at all. All Russian literature is charged with a revolutionary spirit; but there is the same difference between those authors whose aim is political and those who merely speak of Russia's wounds when occasion offers, that there is between those who are licentious and those who are simply open and candid. And by this I do not mean to compare the nihilist writers with licentious ones, nor to convey any stigma by my words. I merely say that when literature deliberately attacks established society, the instinct of self-preservation obliges the latter to defend itself even to persecuting its adversary.

II.

ORIGIN OF THE INTELLECTUAL REVOLUTION.

WHENCE came the revolutionary element in Russia? From the Occident, from France, from the negative, materialist, sensualist philosophy of the Encyclopædia imported into Russia by Catherine II.; and later from Germany, from Kantism and Hegelianism, imbibed by Russian youth at the German universities, and which they diffused throughout their own country with characteristic Sclav impetuosity. By "Pure Reason" and transcendental idealism, Herzen and Bakunine, the first apostles of nihilism, were inspired. But the ideas brought from Europe to Russia soon allied themselves with an indigenous or possibly an Oriental element; namely, a sort of quietist fatalism, which leads to the darkest and most despairing pessimism. On the whole, nihilism is rather a philosophical conception of the sum of life than a purely democratic and revolutionary movement. Since the beginning of this century Europe has seen mobs and revolutions, dynasties wrecked and governments overturned; but these were political disturbances, and not the result of mind diseased or anguish of soul.

Nihilism had no political color about it at the beginning. During the decade between 1860 and 1870 the youth of Russia was seized with a sort of fever for negation, a fierce antipathy toward everything that was, — authorities, institutions, customary ideas, and old-fashioned dogmas. In Turguenief's novel, "Fathers and Sons," we meet with Bazarof, a froward, ill-mannered, intolerable fellow, who represents this type. After 1871 the echo of the Paris Commune and emissaries of the Internationals crossed the frontier, and the nihilists began to bestir themselves, to meet together clandestinely, and to send out propaganda. Seven years later they organized an era of terror, assassination, and explosions. Thus three phases have followed upon one another,— thought, word, and deed,—along that road which is never so long as it looks, the road that leads from the word to the act, from Utopia to crime.

And yet nihilism never became a political party as we understand the term. It has no defined creed or official programme. The fulness of its despair embraces all negatives and all acute revolutionary forms. Anarchists, federalists, cantonalists, covenanters, terrorists, all who are unanimous in a desire to sweep away the present order, are grouped under the ensign of *nihil*.

The frenzy which thus moves a whole people to tear their hair and rend their garments has at bottom an element of passionate melancholy born of just and noble aspirations crushed by fatal circumstances. We have seen what Nature and history have made of Russia,—a nation civilized by violence, whose natural and harmonious development was checked, and which was isolated from Europe as soon as the ruling powers perceived the dangers likely to ensue from communication therewith. The impulse of youth toward the unknown and the new, toward vague dreams and abstractions, was thus exasperated; and from out the seminaries, universities, and schools, from the ranks of the nobility and from the bosom of the literature, there arose a host composed of women hungering for the ideal, and young students, poor in pocket and position, who gave themselves up to a Bohemian sort of life well calculated to set at nought society and the world in general. A Russian friend once told me that seeing a *mujik* looking very dejected and melancholy he asked what was the matter, and received answer, " Sir, we are a sick people." His reply defines the whole race ; and of all the explanations of nihilism, that which describes it as a pathological condition of the nation is perhaps the most accurate.

One must be prudent, however, in calling an intellectual phenomenon based upon historical reasons a sickness or dementia ; and above all one must not confound the mental exaltation of the enthusiast with the vagaries of the unsound mind. We do not allow ourselves to call him a fool who does not think as we do, nor even him who leaves the beaten common track for dizzy heights above our ken. No reformer or other great man, however, has escaped the insinuation of foolishness, not even Saint Francis of Assisi, who openly professed idiocy. But we have a kind of sympathy for madness of a speculative character, — the sort of lunacy which makes mankind dream sometimes that material good does not entirely satisfy, that makes it yearn anxiously for something that it may never obtain on this earth.

To begin with, is nihilism pure negation? No. Pure negation conceives nothing further, and whatever it denies it affirms at the same time. Nihilism, or to use their own term, Russian *intelligence*, contains the germs of social renovation; and before referring to its political history I will explain some of its strange and curious doctrines.

III.

WOMAN AND THE FAMILY.

AMONG the most important of the nihilist doctrines is that which refers to the condition of woman and the constitution of the family; and the attempt radically to modify things so guarded and so sacred presupposes an extraordinary power in the moving principle. The state of woman in Russia has been far more bitter and humiliating than in the rest of Europe; she wore her face covered with the Oriental veil until an empress dared to cast it aside, — to the great horror of the court; among the peasants she was a beast of burden; among the nobles an odalisque; in the most enlightened classes of society the whip hung at the head of the bed as a symbol of the husband's authority. The law did not keep her perpetually a minor, as with us, but allowed her to administer her property freely; yet the invisible and unwritten bonds of custom made this freedom illusory. The new ideas have changed all this, however, and to-day the Russian woman is more nearly equal to the man in condition, more free, intelligent, and respected than elsewhere in Europe. Even the peasants, accustomed to bestow a daily allowance of the lash upon their women, are beginning to treat them with more gentleness and regard, for they realize, tardily though certainly, the worth of the ideas of justice deduced from the Gospels, which once planted can never be rooted out. Their conquests are final. A few years hence the conjugal relation in Russia will be based on ideas of equality, fraternity, and mutual respect. I have never gone about preaching emancipation or demanding rights, but I am nevertheless quite capable of appreciating everything that savors of equity.

The great Russian romantic poet, Lermontof, lamented the moral inferiority of the women of his country. "Man," said this Russian Byron, "should not be satisfied with the submission of his slave or the devotion of his dog; he needs the love of a human being who will repay insight for insight, soul for soul." This noble aspiration, derived from the profound Platonic allegory of the two soul-halves that seek each other and thereby find completion, the Russian intelligence desired to realize, and as a step toward it procured participation for woman in intellectual and political life; she, on her part, proved her worth by bringing to nihilism a passionate devotion, absolute faith, and initiative energy. When the early Christians rehabilitated the pagan woman, somewhat the same thing happened, and a tender gratitude toward the gentle Nazarene led virgins and matrons to vie with strong men in the heroism displayed in the amphitheatre.

But in our times the systematic efforts toward female emancipation have a tendency to stumble into absurdities. To show to what an extent conjugal equality has been carried in certain Russian families of humble position, I was told that the wife cooks one day and the husband the next! At the beginning of the reign of Alexander II. the longing for feminine independence was expressed in the wearing of short hair, blue spectacles, and extraordinary dress; in smoking, in scorn of neatness, and the assumption of viragoish and disgusting manners. The serious side of the movement led them on the other hand to study, to throw themselves into every career open to them, to show a brave front in the hospitals of typhus and the plague, to win honors in the clinics, and to practise medicine in the small villages with noble self-abnegation, seriousness, and sagacity.

It is worthy of note, in examining Russian revolutionary tendencies, that political rights are a secondary consideration, and that they go down to the root of the matter, and seek first to reclaim natural rights. In countries that are under parliamentary regimen, half of the human race is judicially and civilly the servant of the other half; while in the classic land of absolutism all parts are equal before the law, especially among the reformatory class, the nobility.

There is one fact in this connection which, though rather dubious on the face of it, is yet so original and typical that it ought not to be omitted. Owing to these modifications in the social condition of women, and also to political circumstances, we are told that one frequently hears in Russia — among the *intelligent* class particularly — of a sort of free unions, having no other bond than the mutual willingness of the contracting parties, and marked by singular characteristics. Some of these unions may be compared to the espousals of Saint Cecilia and her husband, Saint Valerian, or to the nuptials of the legendary 'hero separated by a naked sword from the bride. The Russians call this a fictitious marriage. It sometimes happens that a young girl, bold, determined, and full of a longing for life, — in the social sense of the word, — leaves the paternal roof and takes up her abode under that of another man. Having obtained the liberty and individuality enjoyed by the married woman, the protector and the *protégée* maintain a fraternal friendship mutually and willingly agreed to. In Turguenief's novel, "Virgin Soil," a young lady runs away from her uncle's house with the tutor, a young nihilist poet, with whom she believes herself to be deeply in love; but she finds out that what she really loved and craved was liberty, and the chance to practise her politico-social principles; and as these two runaways live in chastity, the heroine finally, and without any conscientious scruples, marries another poet, also a nihilist, but more practical and intelligent, who has really succeeded in interesting her heart.

Is such a voluntary restriction the result of a hyperæsthesia of the fancy, natural to an age of persecution, in which those who fight for and defend an idea are ready at any moment to go to the gallows for its sake? Is it mere woman's pride demanding for her sex liberty and franchises which she scorns to make use of? Is it a manifestation of an idealist sentiment which is always present in revolutionary outbursts? Is it a consequence of the theory which Schopenhauer preached, but did not practise? Is it Malthusian pessimism which would refuse to provide any more subjects for despotism? Is it a result of the natural coldness of the Scythian? There seems to be no doubt, according to the statement of trustworthy authors, that there are nihilist virgins living promiscuously with students, helping them like sisters, united by this strange understanding. Solovief, who made a criminal attempt on the life of Alexander II., was thus *married*, as was shown at his trial.

Among the young generation of nihilists this sort of union was really an affiliation in devotion to their party. The bride's dower went into the party treasury, her body was consecrated to the worship of the unknown God; and being but slightly bound to his or her nominal spouse, each one went his or her way, sometimes to distant provinces, to propagate and disseminate the good news.

Tikomirov (from whose interesting book I have taken most of my information concerning the constitution of the Russian revolutionary family) seems to think that French authors have not done full justice to the austerity and purity of nihilist customs, and he depicts a charming scene in the home of intelligence, whose members are united and affectionate, where moral and intellectual equality produce solid friendship, precluding tyranny on the one hand and treason on the other; adding that in Russia everybody is convinced of the superiority of this sort of family, and only foreigners think that nihilism undermines the foundations of conjugal union. Is this really true? In any case it seems possible that such a beautiful ideal might be attained to in our Latin societies, given the elevated conception of the Catholic marriage, which makes it a sacrament, were there only a little more equity, toward which it is evident, however, that laws and customs are ever tending.

In speaking of nihilist marriages, it is well to add that in general the Russian revolutionary movement has a pronounced flavor of mysticism, although at first sight it seems an explosion of free-thinking and blasphemy. It is true that nihilist youth laughs at the supernatural, and has been steeped in the crudities of German materialism and in the pliant philosophies of the clinic and the laboratory; but at the same time, whether because of the religious character of the race, or because of a certain exaltation which may be the fruit of a period of stress, the nihilist young people are mystics in their own way, and talk about the martyrs to the cause with an inspired voice and with the unction of a devotee invoking the saints. In proof of this I will give here a nihilist madrigal dedicated to the young heroine in a political trial, Lydia Figuier, who had studied medicine in Zurich and Paris.

"Deep is the impression, O maiden, left by thy enchanting beauty; but more powerful than the charm of thy face is the purity of thy soul. Full of pity is the image of the Saviour, and his divine features are full of compassion; but in the unfathomable depths of thine eyes there is still more love and suffering."

The extremes of this rare sort of fanaticism are still better shown in a famous novel of Tchernichewsky, the hero of which outdoes the Hindu fakirs and Christian anchorites in point of macerations, penances, and austerities. He is offered several kinds of fruit, but he will taste only the apple, which is what the people eat; he fasts in grief and anguish, and one day, in order to accustom himself to bear any sort of trial, he lays himself down upon a cloth thickly studded with nails an inch long, points upward, and there he remains until his blood saturates the ground. Not content with mortifying the flesh in this way, he disposes of all his worldly goods among the poor, and vows never to touch a drop of wine or the lips of woman. This is only the hero of a story-book; yes, but this story endeavors to present a type, an ideal pattern, to which the *new men*, or nihilists, try to conform themselves.

It must be understood that when I say mysticism, I use the word in a generic and not in a theological sense. It seems contradictory to say that an atheist can do and feel like the most fervent believer; but a man may pass a whole lifetime in parrying logic, and yet sometimes what his reason refuses his imagination accepts. There is something in nihilism that recalls the transcendental contradictions of the Hindu philosophies and religions, especially Buddhism; and in Russian brains there is a fermentation of heterodox illumination which is manifested among the common people by sects of tremblers, jumpers, and others, and among the more learned classes by revolutionary mysticism, amorphism, anarchy, and a gloomy and rebellious pessimism. The prophets of the ignorant sects among the people preach many of the revolutionary dogmas, teaching disobedience to all authority, community of goods, social liquidation and free love, yet without political intention; and better educated nihilists, even reactionary minds like Dostoiëwsky, feel the pulse of mystic enthusiasm which runs in the blood. The people are so predisposed to color the language of the political devotee that they were quite satisfied with the answer given by the propagandist Rogatchef to the peasants who asked what he sought among them. He replied, "The true faith."

To the honor of humanity be it said that the most profound emotions it has experienced have been produced by its own thirst for the ideal, and caused by the need of belief, and of feeling in one form or another a religious excitement. It is this element which conquers our sympathy for nihilism; this shows us a young and enthusiastic people given to visions and sublime ardors. To put it more explicitly, I am not passing judgment upon the only revolutionaries just now extant in the world. I have very little liking for political upheavals; but, to the egotistical indifference that afflicts some nations, I believe that I prefer the passionate extremes of nihilism. In politics as in art we want the living.

It will be seen therefore that the people were not irrelevant in confounding nihilism with a religious sect. As far as our rationalist age will admit, the nihilist dissenter resembles the great heretics of the Middle Ages; he has traces of the Millenarian, of Sakya Muni, and of the German pantheists; and he has the blind faith, the hazy transports, the dogmatical and absolute affirmation of the persecuted religious sects, and of esoteric and subterranean beliefs. He adores a divinity without feelings, deaf and primitive, and this adoration is the corner-stone of the nihilist temple. The *mujik* sublimated by Russian literature is the god of nihilism.

IV.

GOING TO THE PEOPLE.

HERE is a passage from Tikomirov's book to illustrate this aspect of Russian revolution:—

"Where is there any sociological theory that can explain the crusade taken up in 1873 by thousands of young men and women determined to *go to the people?* The word crusade is appropriate. Our youths left the bosom of their families; our maidens abandoned the worldly pleasures of life. Nobody thought of his own welfare; the great cause absorbed all attention, and the nervous tension was such that many were able to endure, without injury to health, unusual and dreadful privations. They gave up their past life and all their property, and if any vacillated in offering his fortune to the cause, he was looked upon with pity and contempt. Some renounced official positions and gave all their means, even to thousands of rubles; others, like Prince Krapotkine, from being *savants*, diplomats and opulent, became humble artisans. The prince took to painting doors and windows. Rich heiresses sought occupation as factory operatives, even some who had reigned as belles in aristocratic salons. It was as though, exiled from other classes of society, they found, in turning to the people, their souls' true country."

Do not these words almost seem to describe the beginnings of Christianity in Rome?

The idol takes no notice of his fanatical adorers, nor perhaps does he understand them any better than the peasant-woman of Toboso understood the amorous suit with which Don Quixote wooed her malformed and dishevelled person. The Russian peasant cannot make anything of theories and apotheoses evolved from an intellectual condition amounting to rapturous frenzy. "Oh that I might die," exclaims a devout nihilist, "and that my blood like a drop of hot lead could burn and arouse the people!" This thirst for martyrdom is common, but above all is the anxiety to be amalgamated with the people, to know them, and if possible to infuse them with the enthusiasm they feel themselves.

It requires more courage to do what Russians call *going to the people*, than to bear exile or the gallows. In our society, which boasts of its democracy, the very equalization of classes has strengthened the individual instinct of difference, and especially the aristocrats of mind, the writers and thinkers, have become terribly nervous, finicky, and inimical to the plebeian smell, to the extent that even novels which describe the common people with sincerity and truth displease the public taste. Yet the nihilists, a select company from the point of view of intellectual culture, go, like apostles, in search of the poor in spirit, the ignorant and the humble. The sons of families belonging to the highest classes, alumni of universities, leave fine clothes and books, dress like peasants, and mix with factory hands, so as to know them and to teach them; young ladies of fine education return from a foreign tour and accept with the utmost contentment situations as cooks in manufacturers' houses, so as to be able to study the labor question in their workshops. We find very curious instances of this in Turguenief's novel "Virgin Soil." The heroine, Mariana, a nihilist, in order to learn how the people live, and to *simplify herself* (this is a sacramental term), helps a poor peasant-woman in her domestic duties. Here we have the way of the world reversed: the educated learns of the ignorant, and in all that the peasant-woman does or says the young lady finds a crumb of grace and wisdom. "We do not wish to teach the people," she explains, "we wish to serve them." "To serve them?" replies the woman, with hard practicality. "Well, the best way to serve them is to teach them." Equally fruitless are the efforts of Mariana's *fictitious husband*, or *husband by free grace*, as the peasant-woman calls him, — the poet and dreamer Nedjanof, who thinks himself a nihilist, but in the bottom of his soul has the aristocratic instincts of the artist. Here is the passage where he presents himself to Mariana dressed in workman's clothes: —

"Mariana uttered an exclamation of surprise. At first she did not know him. He wore an old caftan of yellowish drill, short-waisted, and buttoned with small buttons; his hair was combed in the Russian style, with the part in the middle; a blue kerchief was tied around his neck; he held in his hand an old cap with a torn visor, and his feet were shod with undressed calfskin."

Mariana's first act on seeing him in this guise is to tell him that he is indeed ugly, after which disagreeable piece of information, and a shudder of repugnance at the smell of his greasy cap and dirty sleeves, they provide themselves with pamphlets and socialist proclamations and start out on their Odyssey among the people, hoping to meet with ineffable sufferings. He would be no less glad than she of a heroic sacrifice, but he is not content with a grotesque farce; and the girl is indignant when Solomine, her professor in nihilism, tells her that her duty actually compels her to wash the children of the poor, to teach them the alphabet, and to give medicine to the sick. "That is for Sisters of Charity," she exclaims, inadvertently recognizing a truth; the Catholic faith contains all ways of loving one's neighbor, and none can ever be invented that it has not foreseen. But the human type of the novel is Nedjanof, although the nihilists have sought to deny it. There is one very sad and real scene in which he returns drunk from one of his propagandist excursions, because the peasants whom he was haranguing compelled him to drink as much as they. The poor fellow drinks and drinks, but he might as well have thrown himself upon a file of bayonets. He comes home befuddled with *wodka*, or perhaps more so with the disgust and nausea which the brutish and mal-odorous people produced in him. He had never fully believed in the work to which he had consecrated himself: now it is no longer scepticism, it is invincible disgust that takes hold upon his soul, urging him to despair and suicide. The lament of his lost revolutionary faith is contained in the little poem entitled "Dreaming," which I give literally, as follows: —

"It was long since I had seen my birthplace, but I found it not at all changed. The deathlike sleep, intellectual inertia, roofless houses, ruined walls, mire and stench, scarcity and misery, the insolent looks of the oppressed peasants, — all the same! Only in sleeping, we have outstripped Europe, Asia, and the whole world. Never did my dear compatriots sleep a sleep so terrible!

"Everything sleeps: wherever I turn, in the fields, in the cities, in carriages, in sleighs, day and night, sitting or walking; the merchant and the functionary, and the watchman in the tower, all sleep in the cold or in the heat! The accused snores and the judge dozes; the peasants sleep the sleep of death; asleep they sow and reap and grind the corn; father, mother, and children sleep! The oppressed and the oppressor sleep equally well!

"Only the gin-shop is awake, with eyes ever open!

"And hugging to her breast a jug of fire-water, her face to the pole, her feet to the Caucasus, thus sleeps and dreams on forever our Mother, Holy Russia!"

To all nihilist intents and purposes, particularly to those of a political character, the masses are apparently asleep. Many eloquent anecdotes refer to their indifference. A young lady propagandist, who served as cook on a farm, confesses that the peasants spitefully accused her of taking bread from the poor. In order to get them to take their pamphlets and leaflets, the nihilists present them as religious tracts, adorning the covers with texts of Scripture and pious mottoes and signs. Only by making good use of the antiquated idea of distribution (of goods) have they any chance of success; it is of no use to talk of autonomous federations, or to attack the emperor, who has the people on his side.

The active nihilists are always young people, and this is reason enough why they are not completely discouraged by the sterility of their efforts. Old age abhors fruitless endeavors, and better appreciating the value of life, will not waste it in tiresome experiments. And this contrast between the ages, like that between the seasons, is nowhere so sharp as in Russia; nowhere else is the difference of opinions and feelings between two generations so marked. Some one has called nihilism a disease of childhood, like measles or diphtheria; perhaps this is not altogether erroneous, not only as regards individuals but also as regards society, for vehemence and furious radicalism are the fruit of historical inexperience, of the political youth of a nation. The precursor of nihilism, Herzen, said, with his brilliant imagery and vigor of expression, that the Russia of the future lay with a few insignificant and obscure young folks who could easily hide between the earth and the soles of the autocrat's boots; and the poet Mikailof, who was sentenced to hard labor in 1861, and subsequently died under the lash, exclaimed to the students, "Even in the darkness of the dungeon I shall preserve sacredly in my heart of hearts the incomparable faith that I have ingrafted upon the new generation."

It is sad to see youth decrepit and weary from birth, without enthusiasm or ambition for anything. It is more natural that the sap should overflow, that a longing for strife and sacrifice, even though foolish and vain, should arise in its heart. This truth cannot be too often repeated: to be enthusiastic, to be full of life, is not ridiculous; but our pusillanimous doctrine of disapproval is ridiculous indeed, especially in life's early years, — as ridiculous as baldness at twenty, or wrinkles and palsy at thirty. Besides, we must recognize something more than youthful ardor in nihilism, and that is, sympathetic disinterestedness. The path of nihilism does not lead to brilliant position or destiny: it may lead to Siberia or to the gibbet.

V.

HERZEN AND THE NIHILIST NOVEL.

But it is time to mention some of the precursors of nihilism. First of all there is Alexander Herzen, a brilliant, paradoxical writer, a great visionary, a keen satirist, the poet of denial, a romanticist and idealist to his own sorrow, and, in the bottom of his soul, sceptical and melancholy. Herzen was born in Moscow in the year of the Fire, and his mind began to mature about the time the December conspirators forced Nicholas I. into trembling retirement. He was wont to say that he had seen the most imposing personification of imperial power, had grown up under the shadow of the secret police and panted in its clutches. Charmed by the philosophical doctrines of Hegel and Feuerbach, which were then superseding the French, he became a socialist and a revolutionary. Just at the time when to have a constitution was the ideal and the dream of the Latin peoples, who were willing to tear themselves to pieces to obtain it, this Sclav was writing that a constitution was a miserable contract between a master and his slaves! Herzen was but a little more than twenty years old when he was sent to Siberia. On his return from exile he found at home a mental effervescence, a Germanic and idealist current in the wake of the eminent critic Bielinsky, Sclavophiles singing hymns in praise of national life and repudiating European civilization which was in turn defended by the so-called Occidentals; and lastly he found a set of literary innovators who formed the famous *natural school*, at the head of which was the great Gogol. Herzen fell into this whirl of ideas, and his æsthetic doctrines and advanced Hegelianism had great influence, and after some more serious works he published his celebrated novel, "Who is to Blame?"—a masterly effort, which gained him immense renown in Russia. It was masterly more by reason of the popularity it achieved than by its literary merit, for Herzen is, after all, not to be counted among the chief novel-writers of Russia. Herzen was born to point the way to a social Utopia rather than the road to pure Beauty. He invented new phases of civilization, societies transformed by the touch of a magic wand. The star of Proudhon was at this time in the ascendant, and Herzen, attracted by its brilliancy, left his country never to return; but he did not on this account cease to exercise a great influence upon her destinies, so great, indeed, that some profess to think that had Herzen never lived, nihilism would have perished in the bud.

Herzen hailed with delight the French revolution of 1848. He expected to behold a social liquidation, but he saw instead only a conservative republic,—a change of form. Then he cried out in savage despair, and his words have become the true nihilist war-cry: "Let the old world perish! Let chaos and destruction come upon it! Hail, Death! Welcome to the Future!"

To sweep away the past with one stroke became his perennial aspiration. He drew a vivid picture of a secret tribunal which every *new man* carries within himself, to judge, condemn, and guillotine the past; he described how a man, fearful of following up his logical conclusions, after citing before this tribunal the Church, the State, the family, the good, and the evil, might make an effort to save a rag of the worn-out yesterday, unable to see that the lightest weight would prove a hindrance to his passage from the old world to the new. "There is a remarkable likeness between logic and terror," he said. "It is not for us to pluck the fruits of the past, but to destroy them, to persecute them, to judge them, to unmask them, and to immolate them upon the altars of the future. Terror sentenced human beings; it concerns us to judge institutions, demolish creeds, put no faith in old things, unsettle every interest, break every bond, without mercy, without leniency, without pity."

This was his programme: Not to civilize or to progress, but to obliterate, to demolish; to replace what he called the senile barbarity of the world with a juvenile barbarity; "to go to the very limits of absurdity," — these are his own words. They contain the sum of nihilism; they include the pessimist despair, and the foolish proscription of art, beauty, and culture, which to an artistic mind is the greatest crime that can be laid at the door of any political or philosophical doctrine. A tendency that aspires to overthrow the altar sacred to the Muses and the Graces can never prevail.

Herzen went to London, established a press for the dissemination of political writings in Russia, and organized a secret society for Russian refugees, among whom he counted Bakunine; and having refused to return to his country, he founded a singular paper called "The Bell" (*Kolokol*), of which thousands of copies, though strictly prohibited by the censor, crossed the frontier. They were distributed and read on every hand, and a copy was regularly placed, by invisible hands, in the chamber of the emperor, who devoured it no less eagerly than his faithful subjects. From the pages of this illegal publication the sovereign learned of secret intrigues in his palace, of plots among his high officials, and scandalous stories reported by the socialist refugee with incredible accuracy. By the side of these evidences of dexterity and cleverness, some of the stratagems recounted of the times of our own Carlist war seem mere child's play.

As the precursor of nihilism Herzen excites great interest, but there is much to be said of Tchernichewsky and Bakunine. It is said that the latter's influence was more felt abroad than at home, and that he fanned the activity of the Internationalist societies, and of the Swiss, Italian, and Spanish laboring classes. Be that as it may, Bakunine was a classic type of the conspirator by profession, — in love with his dangerous work. He adopted as his motto that to destroy is to create. Caussidière saw him and watched him during the insurrections in Paris, and exclaimed, "What a man! The first day of the revolution he is a treasure; on the second we must shoot him!" Paris was not the only witness of his feats; he fought like a lion at the barricades in Dresden, and was elected dictator; he took an active part in the Polish insurrection; he quite outshone Carl Marx in the International, and with him originated the anarchist faction, and that last grade of revolution, amorphism. As for Tchernichewsky, he is considered the great master and inspirer of contemporary nihilism, his principal claim to such a place being based on a novel; and at the bottom of the Russian revolution we shall always find the epic fictions of our day exerting a powerful influence.

With Herzen's novel the tendencies of nihilism were first revealed; with Tchernichewsky's they became fixed and decisive. Novels of Gogol and Turguenief overthrew serfdom, and novels of Turguenief, Dostoiëwsky, Tolstoï, Gontcharof, and Tchedrine are the documents which historians will consult hereafter when the great contest between the revolution and the old society shall be written. When Tchernichewsky wrote his famous novel, he had already tried his hand at various public questions, had made a compilation from the "Political Economy" of John Stuart Mill, and was a prisoner on the charge of organizing the revolutionary propaganda in Russia along with Herzen, Ogaref, and Bakunine, who were refugees in London. Before setting out to suffer his sentence of fifteen years' imprisonment and perpetual residence in Siberia, he was tied to a stake in a public square of St. Petersburg, and after the reading of the sentence a sword was broken over his head. What a blow was dealt at absolute power by this man, shut up, annihilated, suppressed, and civilly dead! Happy the cause that hath martyrs!

His novel produced an indescribable sensation. The nihilists were inclined to resent Turguenief's "Fathers and Sons," whose hero, the materialist Bazarof, represented the new generation, or, according to them, caricatured it. Tchernichewsky's book was considered to be a faithful picture, and a model besides for the party; it was the nihilists painted by one of themselves, so to speak. Although it is tedious and inconsistent in its arguments, the book shows much talent and a fertile imagination; the author declares that it is his purpose to stereotype the personality of the *new man*, who is but an evanescent type, a sign of the times, destined to disappear with the epoch he has initiated. Writing about the year 1850, he says, "Six years ago there were no such men; three years ago they were little noticed, and now — but what matters what is thought of them now? Soon enough they will hear the cry, Save us! and whatever they command shall be done." Farther on he says that these *new men* in turn shall disappear to the last man; and after a long time men shall say, "Since the days of those men things go on better, although not entirely well yet." Then the type shall reappear again in larger numbers and in greater perfection, and this will continue to happen until men say, "Now we are doing well!" And when this hour arrives, there will be no special types of humanity, there will be no *new men*, for all shall realize the largest sum of perfection possible. Such is the theory of this famous martyr, and it is certainly as original as it is curious.

The admirers of Tchernichewsky's novel compare it to "The City of the Sun," by Campanella, "Utopia," by Sir Thomas More, "The Journey to Icaria," by Cabet, and the phalansterian sketches by Fourier's disciples. This comparison is alone sufficient to decide the rivalry in favor of Turguenief; for the Siberian exile wrought only in the interest of socialist propaganda, while the author of "Virgin Soil," whether accurate or not in detail, was a consummate artist. Only political excitement can dictate certain judgments and decisions. If I speak now more at length of the exile's novel, it is for the sake of its representative value, and as a reflection of nihilism in literature. The title is, "What to do?" The author wishes to solve the problem put by Herzen in the title to his novel, "Who is to blame?" and under the guise of a love-quarrel he delineates the ideal of the contemporary generation represented by two favorite characters, the two classic types of the nihilist novel, — the student of medicine, a *new man*, saturated with science and German metaphysics, and a brave girl longing to be *initiated* and thirsting to consecrate herself to some lofty cause. Among other curiosities there is a nihilist husband, who, on discovering that his wife is enamoured of somebody else, calculates his moral sufferings as equivalent to the excitement produced by four cupfuls of strong coffee, and he therefore takes two morphine pills and declares that he feels better! In spite of being prohibited by the censor, this novel, as might be expected, had a great success; the editions multiplied clandestinely; the heroine's type became immensely popular; the young girls took to the study of medicine with an enthusiasm and a will to which I can personally testify; and if report be true, a part of the new ideas concerning conjugal equality and the constitution of the family proceeded from this novel. The popularity of the author, glorified by the halo of his sufferings and imprisonment, far superseded that of Herzen.

Materialism and positivism soon came also to replace the visions of Herzen; for when Alexander II. opened the frontiers which the inflexible Nicholas had closed, the students brought home new idols from the German universities. Schopenhauer and Buchner superseded Hegel and Feuerbach. Schopenhauer, with his pessimism, his theory of Nirvana and universal annihilation, arrived just in time to foster the germs of fatalism dormant within the Russian soul; and Buchner, by means of his very superficial but eloquent book, was also in season to offer an accessible, clear, and popular formula to unthinking minds and negative or indolent temperaments. "Force and matter" was for a time the Bible of Russian students. It will be readily seen that the revolutionary formula and methods in Russia always came from abroad; but they met with tendencies which were unexpected, even though they proved favorable to development. The philosophy of nihilism was drawn from Western sources, no doubt; yet this phenomenon made its appearance only in Russia, a land predisposed to realism and mysticism, to brutality and languor, and above all to melancholy limitless as its plains.

We are told of the now famous saying of a nihilist, who, being asked his doctrines, replied, "To see earth and heaven, Church and State, God and king, and to spit upon them all!" Although the verb to *spit* is not so offensive in Russia as here, and is rather a sign of repugnance than of insult, such a reply contains the sum of negative nihilism; and negation, the critical period, cannot last longer than the despairing sigh of the dying. The active phase of nihilism, the reign of terror, passed by quickly, and now the party is beginning to lay aside its ferocious radicalism and deal with realities.

VI.

THE REIGN OF TERROR.

THE reign of terror was short but tragic. We have seen that the active nihilists were a few hundred inexperienced youths without position or social influence, armed only with leaflets and tracts. This handful of boys furiously threw down the gauntlet of defiance at the government when they saw themselves pursued. Resolved to risk their heads (and with such sincerity that almost all the associates who bound themselves to execute what they called *the people's will* have died in prison or on the scaffold), they adopted as their watchword *man for man.* When the sanguinary reprisals fell upon Russia from one end to the other, the frightened people imagined an immense army of terrorists, rich, strong, and in command of untold resources, covering the empire. In reality, the twenty offences committed from 1878 to 1882, the mines discovered under the two capitals, the explosions in the station at Moscow and in the palace at St. Petersburg, the many assassinations, and the marvellous organization which could get them performed with circumstances so dramatic and create a mysterious terror against which the power of the government was broken in pieces, — all this was the work of a few dozens of men and women seemingly endowed with ubiquitousness, so rapid and unceasing their journeys, and so varied the disguises, names, and stratagems they made use of to bewilder and confound the police. It was whispered that millions of money were sent in from abroad, that there were members of the Czar's family implicated in the conspiracy, that there was an unknown chief, living in a distant country, who managed the threads of a terrible executive committee which passed judgment in the dark, and whose decrees were carried out instantly. Yet there were only a few enthusiastic students, a few young girls ready to perform any service, like the heroine of Turguenief's "Shadows;" a few thousand rubles, each contributing his share; and, after all, a handful of determined people, who, to use the words of Leroy-Beaulieu, had made a covenant with death. For a strong will, like intelligence or inspiration, is the patrimony of the few; and so, just as ten or twelve artist heads can modify the æsthetic tendency of an age, six or eight intrepid conspirators are enough to stir up an immense empire.

After Karakozof's attempt upon the life of the Czar (the first spark of discontent), the government augmented the police and endowed Muravief, who was nicknamed *the Hangman*, with dictatorial powers. In 1871 the first notable political trial was held upon persons affiliated with a secret society. Persecutions for political offences are a great mistake. Maltreatment only inspires sympathy. After a few such trials the doors had to be closed; the public had become deeply interested in the accused, who declared their doctrines in a style only comparable to the acts of the early Christian martyrs. Who could fail to be moved at the sight of a young woman like Sophia Bardina, rising modestly and explaining before an audience tremulous with compassion her revolutionary ideas concerning society, the family, anarchy, property, and law? Power is almost always blind and stupid in the first moments of revolutionary disturbances. In Russia men risked life and security as often by acts of charity toward conspirators as by conspiracy itself. In Odessa, which was commanded by General Totleben, the little blond heads of two children appeared between the prison bars; they were the children of a poor wretch who had dropped five rubles into a collection for political exiles, and these two little ones were sentenced to the deserts of Siberia with their father. And the poet Mikailof chides the revolutionaries with the words: "Why not let your indignation speak, my brothers? Why is love silent? Is our horrible misfortune worthy of nothing more than a vain tribute of tears? Has your hatred no power to threaten and to wound?"

The party then armed itself, ready to vindicate its political rights by means of terror. The executive committee of the revolutionary socialists — if in truth such a committee existed or was anything more than a triumvirate — favored this idea. Spies and fugitives were quickly executed. The era of sanguinary nihilism was opened by a woman, the Charlotte Corday of nihilism, — Vera Zasulitch. She read in a newspaper that a political prisoner had been whipped, contrary to law, — for corporal punishment had been already abolished, — and for no worse cause than a refusal to salute General Trepof; she immediately went and fired a revolver at his accuser. The jury acquitted her, and her friends seized her as she was coming out of court, and spirited her away lest she should fall into the hands of the police; the emperor thereupon decreed that henceforth political prisoners should not be tried by jury. Shortly after this the substitute of the imperial deputy at Kief was fired upon in the street; suspicion fell upon a student; all the others mutinied; sixteen of them were sent into exile. As they were passing through Moscow their fellow-students there broke from the lecture-halls and came to blows with the police. Some days later the rector of the University of Kief, who had endeavored to keep clear of the affair, was found dead upon the stairs; and again later, Heyking, an officer of the *gendarmerie*, was mortally stabbed in a crowded street. The clandestine press declared this to have been done by order of the executive committee; and it was not long before the chief of secret police of St. Petersburg received a very polite notice of his death-sentence, which was accomplished by another dagger, and the clandestine paper, "Land and Liberty," said by way of comment, "The measure is filled, and we gave warning of it." Months passed without any new assassinations; but in February, 1879, Prince Krapotkine, governor of Karkof, fell by the hand of a masked man, who fired two shots and fled, and no trace of him was to be found, though sentence of death against him was announced upon the walls of all the large towns of Russia. The brother of Prince Krapotkine was a furious revolutionary, and conducted a socialist paper in Geneva at that time. In March it fell to the turn of Colonel Knoup of the *gendarmerie*, who was assassinated in his own house, and beside him was found a paper with these words: " By order of the Executive Committee. So will we do to all tyrants and their accomplices." A pretty nihilist girl killed a man at a ball; it was at first thought to be a love-affair, but it was afterward found out that the murderess did the deed by order of the executive committee, or whatever the hidden power was which inspired such acts.

On the 25th of this same March a plot against the life of the new chief of police, General Drenteln, was frustrated, and the walls of the town then flamed with a notice that revolutionary justice was about to fall upon one hundred and eighty persons. It rained crimes, — against the governor of Kief, against Captain Hubbenet, against Pietrowsky, chief of police, who was riddled with wounds in his own room; and lastly on the 14th of April Solovief attempted the life of the Czar, firing five shots, none of which took effect. On being caught, the would-be assassin swallowed a dose of poison, but his suicide was also unsuccessful. Solovief, however, had reached the heights of nihilism; he had dared to touch the sacred person of the Czar. He was the ideal nihilist: he had renounced his profession, determined to *go with the people*, and became a locksmith, wearing the artisan's dress; he was married *mystically*, and by *free grace* or *free will*, and it was said that he was a member of the terrible executive committee. He suffered death on the gallows with serenity and composure, and without naming his accomplices. "Land and Liberty" approved his acts by saying, "We should be as ready to kill as to die; the day has come when assassination must be counted as a political motor." From that day Alexander II. was a doomed man, and his fatal moment was not far off. The revolutionaries were determined to strike the government with terror, and to prove to the people that the sacred emperor was a man like any other, and that no supernatural charm shielded his life. At the end of 1879 and the beginning of 1880 two lugubrious warnings were forced upon the emperor: first, the mine which wrecked the imperial train, and then the explosion which threw the dining-room of the palace in ruins, which catastrophe he saw with his own eyes. About this time the office of a surreptitious paper was attacked, the editors and printers of which defended themselves desperately; alarmed by this significant event, the emperor intrusted to Loris Melikof, who was a liberal, an almost omnipotent dictatorship. The conciliatory measures of Melikof somewhat calmed the public mind; but just as the Czar had convened a meeting for the consideration of reforms solicited by the general opinion, his own sentence was carried out by bombs.

It is worthy of note that both parties (the conservative and the revolutionary) cast in each other's face the accusation of having been the first to inflict the death-penalty, which was contrary to Russian custom and law. If Russia does not deserve quite so appropriately as Spain to be called the country of *vice versas*, it is nevertheless worth while to note how she long ago solved the great juridical problem upon which we are still employing tongue and pen so busily. Not only is capital punishment unknown to the Russian penal code, but since 1872 even perpetual confinement has been abolished, twenty years being the maximum of imprisonment; and this even to-day is only inflicted upon political criminals, who are always treated there with greater severity than other delinquents. Before the celebrated Italian criminalist lawyer, Beccaria, ever wrote on the subject, the Czarina Elisabeth Petrowna had issued an edict suppressing capital punishment. The terrible Muscovite whip probably equalled the gibbet, but aside from the fact that it had been seldom used, it was abolished by Nicholas I. If we judge of a country by its penal laws, Russia stands at the head of European civilization. The Russians were so unaccustomed to the sight of the scaffold, that when the first one for the conspirators was to be built, there were no workmen to be found who knew how to construct it.

VII.

THE POLICE AND THE CENSOR.

It is not easy to say whether the government was ill-advised in confronting the terrors of nihilism with the terrors of authority. Public executions are contageous in their effect, and blood intoxicates. The nihilists, even in the hour of death, did not neglect their propaganda, and held up to the people their dislocated wrists as evidences of their tortures. One must put one's self in the place of a government menaced and attacked in so unusual a manner. Certain extreme measures which are the fruit of the stress of the moment are more excusable than the vacillating system commonly practised from time immemorial, and which is foster-mother to professional demagogues, and dynamiters by vocation and preference.

The police as organized in Russia seem to inspire greater horror even than the nihilist atrocities. In the face of judicial reforms there exists an irresponsible tribunal, called the Third Section of the Imperial Chancellorship. The worst of this kind of arbitrary and antipathetic institutions is that imagination attributes many more iniquities to them than they in reality commit. Russian written law declares that no subject of the Czar can be condemned without a public trial; but the special police has the right to arrest, imprison, and make way with, rendering no account to any one. Thus absolute power leaps the barriers of justice. It must be acknowledged that the dark ways of the special police only reflected those of their nihilist adversary. Nowhere in the world, however, is the police so hated; nowhere do they perform their work in so irritating a manner as in Russia; and the public, far from assisting them, as in England and France, fights and circumvents them. The proneness to secret societies in Russia is the result of the perpetual and odious tyranny of the police. The Russian lives in clandestine association like a fish in water; so much so that after the fall of Loris Melikof the reactionaries were no less eager for it than the nihilists, and bound themselves together under the name of the Holy League, taking as a model the revolutionary executive committee, and even including the death-sentence in their rules.

War without quarter was declared, and the police

organized a counter-terror characterized by impeachment, suspicion, espionage, and inquisition. There were domiciliary visitations; every one was obliged to take notice whether any illegal meetings were held in his neighborhood, or any proscribed books or explosive materials were to be seen; no posters were allowed to be put on the walls, and every one was expected to aid the arrest of any suspicious person; a vigilant watch was kept upon Russian refugees; the rigors of confinement were enforced; and all this made the police utterly abhorred, even in a country accustomed to endure them as a traditional institution since the last of the Ruriks and the first of the Romanoffs.

The chief of the Third Section became a power in the land. The Section worked secretly and actively. The chief and the emperor maintained incessant communication, and the former was made a member of the cabinet, and could arrest, imprison, exile, and put out of the way, whomever he pleased. During the reign of the kind-hearted Alexander II. his power declined for a while, until nihilist plots and manœuvres caused it to be redoubled. There was a struggle unto death between two powers of darkness, from which the police came out beaten, having been unable to save the lives of their chief and the sovereign.

While the Third Section attacked personal security and liberty, the censorship, more intolerable still, hemmed in the spirit and condemned to a death by inanition a young people hungry for literature and science, for plays, periodicals, and books. Mutilated as it is, the newspaper is bread to the soul of the Russian. The Russian press, like all the obstacles that absolute power finds in its way, was founded by one of their imperial civilizers, Peter the Great, and it maintained a purely literary character until the reign of Alexander II., when it took a political form. Under the iron hand of the censor, the Russian press has learned the manner and artifices of the slave; in allusions, insinuations, retentions, and half-meanings it is an adept, for only so can it convey all that it is forbidden to speak. It must emigrate and recross the frontier as contraband in order to speak freely.

The censor lies ever in ambush like a mastiff ready to bite; and sometimes its teeth clinch the most inoffensive words on the page, the most innocent page in the book, the librettos of operas, as for example "The Huguenots" and "William Tell." In 1855 certain literary works were exempted from the previous censure, but this beneficence was not extended to the periodical press. The newspapers of St. Petersburg and Moscow were open to a choice between the new and old systems, between submitting to the rule of the censor and a deluge of denunciations, seizures, suspensions, and suppressions; and they willingly chose the former. So the Russian press exists under an entirely arbitrary sufferance, and according as the political scales rise and fall they are allowed to-day what was prohibited yesterday, and sometimes their very means of sustenance are cut off by an embargo on certain numbers or the proscription of advertisements. If a liberal minister is to the fore, times are prosperous; if there is a reaction, they are crushed to death. This accounts for the popularity of the secret press, which is at work even in buildings belonging to the crown, in seminaries and convents, and in the very laboratory of dynamite bombs.

Books are as much harassed as periodicals. The Russians, being very fond of everything foreign, sigh for books from abroad, especially those that deal with political and social questions; but the censor has custom-houses at the frontier, and the officials, with the usual perspicacity of literary monitors, finally let slip that which may prove most dangerous and subversive, and exercise their zeal upon the most ingenuous. They have even cut off the *feuilletines* of thousands of French papers, — what patience it must have required to do it! — while Madame Gagneur's novel, "The Russian Virgins," passed unmutilated. I wonder what would be the fate of my peaceful essays should they receive the unmerited honor of translation and reach the frontiers of Muscovy!

As to the foreign reviews, they are submitted to a somewhat amusing process, called the *caviar*. Suspicious passages, if they escape the scissors, get an extra dash of printing-ink. Thus the Russian is not even free to read till he goes from home, and by force of dieting he suffers from frequent mental indigestion, and the weakest sort of *spirits* goes to his head!

All this goes to prove that if speculative nihilism

is a moral infirmity congenital to the soul of the Russian, active and political nihilism is the fruit of the peculiar situation of the empire. The phrase is stale, but in the present case accurate. Russia is passing through a period of transition. She goes forward to an uncertain future, stumbles and falls; her feet bleed, her senses swim; she has fits of dementia and even of epilepsy. Good intention goes for nought, whether the latent generosity of revolutionaries, or of government and Czar. Where is there a person of nobler desires and projects than Alexander II.? But his great reforms seemed rather to accelerate than to calm the revolutionary fever.

As long as the revolution does not descend from the cultivated classes upon the masses of the people, it must be content with occasional spurts, chimerical attempts, and a few homicides; but if some day the socialist propaganda, which now begins to take effect in the workshops, shall make itself heard in the country villages, and the peasant lend an ear to those who say to him, " Rise, make the sign of the Cross and take thy hatchet with thee," then Russia will show us a most formidable insurrection, and that world of country-folk, patient as cattle, but fanatical and overwhelming in their fury, once let loose, will sweep everything before it. Nothing will appease or satisfy it. The constitutions of Western lands they have already torn in pieces without perusal. Even the revolutionaries would prefer to those illusory statutes a Czar standing at the head of the peasants, and institutions born within their own land. It is said that now, just as the nihilist frenzy is beginning to subside, one can perceive a smouldering agitation among the people manifesting itself occasionally in conflagrations, anti-Semitic outbreaks, and frequent agrarian crimes. What a clouded horizon! What volcanic quakings beneath all that snow! On the one hand the autocratic power, the secular arm, consecrated by time, tradition, and national life; on the other the far-reaching revolution, fanatical and impossible to appease with what has satisfied other nations; and at bottom the cry of the peasants, like the sullen roar of the ocean, for — it is a little thing — the land!

Book III.

RISE OF THE RUSSIAN NOVEL.

I.

THE BEGINNINGS OF RUSSIAN LITERATURE.

FROM this state of anguish, of unrest, of uncertainty, has been brought forth, like amber from the salt sea, a most interesting literature. Into this relatively peaceful domain we are about to penetrate. But before speaking of the novel itself I must mention as briefly as possible the sources and vicissitudes of Russian letters up to the time when they assumed a national and at the same time a social and political character.

I will avoid tiresome details, and the repetition of Russian names which are formidable and harsh to our senses, besides being confusing and at first sight all very much alike, and much given to terminating in *of*, — a syllable which on Russian lips is nevertheless very euphonious and sweet. I will also avoid the mention of books of secondary importance; for as this is not a course of Russian literature, it would be pedantry to refer to more than those I have read from cover to cover. I will mention in passing only a few authors of lesser genius than the four whom Melchior de Voguié very correctly estimates as the perfect national types; namely, Gogol, Turguenief, Dostoiëwsky, and Tolstoï, and I will give only a succinct review of the primitive period, the classicism and romanticism, the satire and comedy antecedent to Gogol, this much being necessary in order to bring out the transformation due to the prodigious genius of this founder of realism, and consummated in the contemporary novel.

Literature, considered not as rhetorical feats or as the art of speaking and writing well, but as a manifestation of national life or of the peculiar inclinations of a people, exists from the time when the spirit of the people is spontaneously revealed in legends, traditions, proverbs, and songs. The fertility of Russian popular literature is well known to students of folk-lore. Critics have demonstrated to us that between the primitive oral, mythical, and poetical literature of Russia and the present novel (which is profoundly philosophical in character, and inspired by that austere muse, the Real) there is as close a relationship as between the gray-haired grandfather who has all his life followed the plough, and his offspring who holds a chair in a university. Russian literature was born beside the Danube, in the fatherland of the Sclavonic people. The various tribes dispersed themselves over the Black Sea, and the Russian Sclavs, following the course of the Dnieper, began to elaborate their heroic mythology with feats of gods and demi-gods against the forces of Nature, and monsters and other fantastic beings. A warlike mode of life and a semi-savage imagination are reflected in their legends and songs. All this period is covered by the *bilinas*, a word which is explained by Russian etymology to mean *songs of the past*. These epics tell of the exploits of ancient warriors who personify the blind and chaotic forces of Nature and the elements. *Esviatogor*, for example, represents a mountain; *Volk* may mean a wolf, a bull, or an ant; there is a godlike tiller of the soil who stands for Russian agriculture, and who is the popular and indigenous hero, in opposition to the fighting and adventurous hero *Volga*, who stands for the ruling classes. Perhaps these *bilinas* and the Finnish Kalevala are the only primitive epics in which the laborer plays a first part and puts the fighting hero into the shade. In these national poems of a people descended from the Scythians, who in the days of Herodotus were proud of calling themselves *farmers* or *laborers*, the two most attractive figures are the heroes of the plough, Mikula and Ilia; it is as though the singers of long ago started the worship of the peasant, which is the dogma of the present novel, or as though the apotheosis of agriculture were an idea rooted in the deepest soil of the national thought of Russia.

Next after this primitive cycle comes the age of chivalry, known under the name of Kief cycle, which has its focus in the Prince Vladimir called the Red Sun; but even in this Round Table epic we find the heroic *mujik*, the giant Cossack, Ilias de Moron. The splendor of the hero-mythical epoch faded after the advent of Christianity, and the heroes of Kief and Novgorod fell into oblivion; one *bilina* tells now "the paladins of Holy Russia disappeared; a great new force that was not of this world came upon them," and the paladins, unable to conquer it, and seeing that it multiplied and became only more powerful with every stroke, were afraid, and ran and hid themselves in the caverns, which closed upon them forever. Since that day there are no more paladins in Holy Russia.

In every *bilina*, and also in songs which celebrate the seed-time, the pagan feast of the summer solstice, and the spring-time, we notice the two characteristics of Russian thought, — a lively imagination and a dreamy sadness, which is most evident in the love-songs. On coming in contact with Christianity the pagan tale became a legend, and the clergy, brought from Byzantium by Valdimir the Baptizer, gave the people the Gospel in the Sclavonic tongue, translated by two Greek brothers, Cyril and Methodius, and the day of liturgical and sacred literature was at hand. The apostles of Christianity arranged the alphabet of thirty-eight letters, which represent all the sounds in the Sclav language, and founded also the grammar and rhetoric. As in every other part of Christendom, these early preachers were the first to enlighten the people, bringing ideas of culture entirely new to the barbarous Sclavonic tribes; and the poor monk, bent over his parchment, writing with a sharp-pointed reed, was the first educator of the nation. In the eleventh century the first Russian literary efforts began to take shape, being, like all early-written literature, of essentially clerical origin and character,— such as epistles, sermons, and moral exhortations. The chief writers of that time were the monk Nestor, the metropolitan Nicephorous, and Cyril the Golden-Mouthed, who imitated the florid Byzantine eloquence. At the side of ecclesiastical literature history was born; the lives of the saints prepared the ground for the chroniclers, and Nestor's Chronicle, the first book on Russian history, was written. The early essays in profane history, which took the form of fables and trenchant sayings disclosing a vein of satire, still smack of the ecclesiastical flavor, although they contain the instincts of a laic and civil literature.

The people had their epic, the clergy accumulated their treasures, but the warriors and knights, who with the sovereign formed a separate society, must have their heroic cycle also; and bards and singers were found to give it to them in fragmentary pieces, among which the most celebrated is the "Song of the Host of Igor," which relates the victories of a prince over the savage tribes of the steppes. The poem is a mixture of pagan and Christian wonders, which is only natural, since in the twelfth century (the era of its composition) Christianity, while triumphant in fact, had not yet succeeded in driving out the old Sclavonic deities.

In the eighth century the Tartar invasion interrupted the course of civil literature. Russia then had

no time for the remembrance of anything but her
disasters, and the Church became again the only
depository of the civilization brought from Byzantium, and of the intellectual riches of the nation; for
the Khans, who destroyed everything else, regarded
the churches and images with superstitious respect.
The little then written expresses the grief of Russia
over her catastrophe, but in sermon form, presenting
it as a punishment from Heaven, and a portent of the
end of the world; it was the universal panic of the
Middle Ages arrived in Russia three centuries late.
Until the fourteenth century there was no revival of
historical narrations in sufficient numbers to show the
preponderance of the epic spirit in the Russian people. In the fifteenth century, for the first time, oral
literature really penetrated into the domain of the
written; but the inevitable and tiresome mediæval
stories of Alexander the Great and the Siege of Troy,
the Thousand and One Nights, and others, entering
by way of Servia and Bulgaria, appear among the
literature of the southern Sclavs; and tales of chivalry
from Byzantium are also rearranged and copied,—
an element of imitation and artificiality which never
took deep root in Russia, however. Aside from some
few tales, the only germs of vitality are to be found
in the apocryphal religious narratives, which were an
early expression of the spirit of mysticism and exegesis, natural to Muscovite thought; and in the songs,
also religious, chanted by pilgrims on their way to
visit the shrines, and by the people also, but probably the work of the monks. These are still sung by

beggars on the streets, and the people listen with delight.

In the sixteenth century there were Maximus the Greek (the Savonarola of Russia), the priest Silvester, author of "Domostroï," a book which was held to contain the model of ancient Russian society, and lastly the Czar, Ivan the Terrible himself, who wrote many notable epistles, models of irony. The songs of the people still flourished, and they were provided with subject-matter by the awful figure and actions of the emperor, who was beloved by the people, because, like Pedro the Cruel of Castile, he dared to bridle the nobles. The popular poet describes him as giving to a potter the insignia and dignity of a Boyar. This tyrant, the most ferocious that humanity ever endured, busied himself with establishing the art of printing in Russia, with the help of Maximus the Greek, who was a great friend of Aldus the Venetian, the famous printer. According to the Metropolitan Macarius, God himself from his high throne put this thought into the heart of the Czar. On the 1st of May, 1564, the first book printed in Russia, "The Acts of the Apostles," made its appearance.

The Russian theatre grew out of the symbolic ceremonies of the church and the representations given by the Polish Jesuits in the colleges; and through Poland, in the seventeenth century, by means of translations or imitations, came also that kind of literary recreations known in France and Italy during the fourteenth century under the name of novels and *facetias*. But these did not intercept the natural course of the national spirit, nor drown the popular voice, — the *duma*, or meditation, the religious canticle, the satire, and especially the incessant reiteration of the *bilinas*, which were now devoted to relating the heroic conquests of the Cossacks. The impulse communicated to Russian thought by Peter the Great at last obliterated the chasm between popular and written literature. Peter established in Russia a school of translators; whatever he thought useful and beneficial he had correctly translated, and then he established the academy. He set up the first regular press and founded the first periodical paper. Not having much confidence in ecclesiastical literature, he commanded that the monks should be deprived of pen, ink, and paper; and on the other hand he revived the theatre, which was apparently dead, and under the influence of his reforms there arose the first Russian writer who can properly be called such, — Lomonosof, the personification of academical classicism, who wrote because he thought it his business, in a well-ordered State, to write incessantly, to polish and perfect the taste, the speech, and even the characters of his fellow-countrymen; he was always a rhetorician, a censor, a corrector, and we seem to see him always armed with scissors and rule, pruning and shaping the myrtles in the garden of literature. The Czar pensioned this ornamental poet, after the fashion of French monarchs, and he in turn bequeathed to his country, of course, a heroic poem entitled "Petriada." His best service to the national literature was in the line of philology; he found a language unrefined and hampered by old Sclavonic forms, and he refined it, softened it, made it more flexible, and ready to yield sweeter melody to those who played upon it thereafter.

Semiramis, in her turn, was not less eager to forward the cause of letters; she had also her palace poet, Derjavine, the Pindar of her court; and not being satisfied with this, her imperial hands grasped the foils and fought out long arguments in the periodicals, to which she contributed for a long time. Woman, just at that time emerging from Oriental seclusion, as during the Renaissance in Europe, manifested an extraordinary desire to learn and to exercise her mind. Catherine became a journalist, a satirist, and a dramatic author; and a lady of her court, the Princess Daschkof, directed the Academy of Sciences, and presided over the Russian Academy founded by Catherine for the improvement and purification of the language, while three letters in the new dictionary are the exclusive work of this learned princess.

Catherine effectively protected her literary men, being convinced that letters are a means of helping the advancement of a barbarous people, in fact the highways of communication; and under her influence a literary Pleiad appeared, among whom were Von-Vizine, the first original Russian dramatist; Derjavine, the official bard and oracle; and Kerakof, the pseudo-classic author of the "Rusiada." Court taste prevailed, and Montesquieu, Voltaire, Rousseau, and

Diderot ruled as intellectual masters of a people totally opposed to the French in their inmost thoughts.

The thing most grateful to the Russian poet in Catherine's time was to be called the Horace or the Pindar of his country; the nobles hid their Muscovite ruggedness under a coat of Voltairian varnish, and even the seminaries resounded with denunciations of *fanaticism* and *horrid superstition*. Other nations have been known to go thus masked unawares. But new currents were undermining the possessions of the Encyclopedists. During the last years of Catherine's reign the theosophical doctrines from Sweden and Germany infiltrated Russia; mysticism brought free-masonry, which finally mounted the throne with Alexander I., the tender friend of the sentimental Valeria; and even had Madame Krudener never appeared to shape in her visions the protest of the Russian soul against the dryness and frivolity of the French philosophers, the fresh lyric quality of Rousseau, Florian, and Bernardin Saint-Pierre would still have flowed in upon the people of the North by means of that eminent man and historian, Karamzine.

Before achieving the title of the Titus Livius of Russia, Karamzine, being a keen intellectual observer of what was going on abroad, founded, by means of a novel, the *emotional school*, declaring that the aim of art is "to pour out floods of grateful impressions upon the realms of the sentimental." This sounds like mere jargon, but such was their mode of speech at the time; and that their spirits demanded just such food is proved by the general use of it, and by the tears that rained upon the said novel, in which the Russian *mujik* appears in the disguise of a shepherd of Arcadia. These innocent absurdities, which were the delight of our own grandmothers, prepared the way for Romanticism, and the appearance of Lermontof and Puchkine.

II.

RUSSIAN ROMANTICISM. — THE LYRIC POETS.

The period of lyric poetry represented by these two excellent poets, Lermontof and Puchkine, was considered the most glorious in Russian literature, and there are yet many who esteem it as such in spite of the contemporary novel. Undoubtedly rhyme can do wonders with this rich tongue in which words are full of color, melody, and shape, as well as ideas. A fine critic has said that Russian poetry is untranslatable, and that one must feel the beauty of certain stanzas of Lermontof and Puchkine sensually, to realize why they are beyond even the most celebrated verses in the world.

At the beginning of the century classicism was in its decline; Russia was leaving her youth behind her, and after 1812 she became totally changed. The Napoleonic wars caused the alliance with Germany, and secret societies of German origin flourished under the favor of the versatile Alexander I.

Weary of the artificial literature imposed by the iron will of Peter the Great, and stirred by a great desire for independence, like all the other nations awakened by Napoleon, Russia held her breath and listened to the birdlike song of the harbingers of a new era, to the great romantic poets who, almost simultaneously and with marvellous accord, burst forth in England, Italy, France, Spain, and Russia. The air was full of melody like the sudden twang of harp-strings in the darkness of the night; and perhaps the autocratic severity of Nicholas I., by forcing attention from public affairs and concentrating it upon literature, was a help rather than a hindrance to this revelation and development.

Alexander Puchkine, the demi-god of Russian verse, carried African as well as Sclavonic blood in his veins, being the grandson of an Abyssinian named Abraham Hannibal, a sort of Othello upon whom Peter the Great bestowed the rank of general and married him to a lady of the court. During the poet's childhood an old servant beguiled him with legends, fables, and popular tales, and the seed fell upon good ground. He left home at the age of fourteen, having quarrelled with all his family and become an out-and-out Voltairian; his professor at the Lyceum — of whom no more needs be said than that he was a brother of Marat — had instilled into his youthful mind the superficial atheism then the fashion; his other tutors declared that this impetuous and fanciful child was throwing away body and soul; yet, when the occasion came, Puchkine remembered all that his old nurse had told him, and found himself with an exquisite æsthetic instinct, in touch with the popular feeling.

When Nicholas I., in December, 1825, mounted the throne vacated by the death of Alexander I. and the renunciation of the Grand-Duke Constantine, Puchkine, then scarcely more than twenty-six years of age, found himself in exile for the second time. His first appearance in public life coincided with the reactionary mood of Alexander I. and the favoritism of the retrogressive minister, Count Arakschef; and the young men from the Lyceum, who had been steeping their souls in liberalism, found themselves defrauded of their expectations of active life, discussions closed, meetings prohibited, and Russia again in a trance of Asiatic immobility. The young nobility began to entertain themselves with conspiracy; and those who had no talent for that, spent their time in drinking and dissipation. Puchkine was as much inclined toward the one as the other. His passionate temperament led him into all sorts of adventures; his eager imagination and his literary tastes incited him to political essays, though under pain of censure. Living amid a whirl of amusement, and coveting an introduction to aristocratic circles, he launched his celebrated poem of "Russia and Ludmilla," which placed him at once at the head of the poets of his day, who had formed themselves into a society called "Arzamas," which was to Russian Romanticism what the Cénacle was to the French, — a centre of attack and defence against classicism; but at length their literary discussions overstepped the forbidden territory of politics, and certain ideas were broached which ended in the conspiracy of December. If Puchkine was not himself a conspirator, he was at least acquainted with the movement; his ode to liberty alarmed the police, and the Czar said to the director of the Lyceum, "Your former pupil is inundating Russia with revolutionary verses, and every boy knows them by heart." That same afternoon the Czar signed the order for Puchkine's banishment, — a great goodfortune for the poet; for had he not been banished he might have been implicated in the conspiracy about to burst forth, and sent to Siberia or to the quicksilver mines. He was expelled from Odessa, which was his first place of confinement, because his Byronic bravado had a pernicious influence upon the young men of the place, and he was sent home to his father, with whom he could come to no understanding whatever. While there he heard of the death of Alexander and the events of December. Upon knowing that his friends were all compromised and under arrest, he started for St. Petersburg, but having met a priest and seen a hare cross his path, he considered these ill omens, and, yielding to superstition, he turned back. Soon afterward he wrote to the new Czar begging reprieve of banishment, which was granted. The Iron Czar sent for him to come to the palace, and held with him a conversation or dialogue which has become famous in the annals of the historians:

"If you had found yourself in St. Petersburg on the 25th of December, where would you have been?" asked Nicholas.

"Among the rebels," answered the poet.

Far from being angry, the sovereign was pleased with his reply, and he embraced Puchkine, saying: "Your banishment is at an end; and do not let fear of the censors spoil your poetry, Alexander, son of Sergius, for I myself will be your censor."

This is not the only instance of this inflexible autocrat's warm-heartedness. More than once his imperial hand stayed the sentence of the censors and gave the wing to genius. Nicholas was not afraid of art, and was, besides, an intelligent amateur of literature. We shall see how he protected even the satire of Gogol. And so, with a royal suavity which softens the most selfish character, Nicholas gained to his side the first poet of Russia, and forever alienated him from the cause for which his friends suffered in gloomy fortresses and in exile, or perished on the scaffold. Puchkine had no other choice than to accept the situation or forfeit his freedom,—to make peace with the emperor or to go and vegetate in some village and bury his talent alive. He chose his vocation as poet, accepted the imperial favor, and returned to St. Petersburg, where he found a remnant of the Arzamas, but now languid and without creative fire. Being restored to his place in high society, he tasted the delights of living in a sphere with which his refined and aristocratic nature was in harmony. He was a poet; he enjoyed the privileges and immunities of a demi-god, the just tribute paid to the productive genius of beauty. And yet at times the pride and independence hushed within his soul stirred again, and he thought with horror upon the hypocrisy of his position as imperial oracle. But he found himself at the height of his glory, doing his best work, seldom annoyed by the censorial scissors, thanks to the Czar; and so, flattered by the throne, the court, and the public, he led to the altar his "brown-skinned virgin," his beautiful Natalia, with whom he was so deeply in love. Having satisfied every earthly desire, he must needs, like Polycrates, throw his ring into the sea.

All his happiness came to a sudden end, and not only his happiness, but his life, went to pay his debt to that high society which had received him with smiles and fair promises. Puchkine's end is as dramatic as any novel. A certain French Legitimist who had been well received by the nobility at St. Petersburg took advantage of the chivalrous customs then in vogue there, to pay court to the poet's beautiful wife, electing her as the lady of his thoughts without disguise. Society protected this little skirmish, and assisted the gallant to meet his lady at every entertainment and in every *salon;* and as Puchkine, though quite unsuspicious, showed plainly that he did not enjoy the game, they amused themselves with exciting and annoying him, ridiculing him, and making him the butt of epigrams and anonymous verses. The marriage of "Dante" — as the adorer of his wife was called — with his wife's sister, far from calming his nerves, only irritated him the more, and he believed it to be a stratagem on the lover's part, a means of approaching the nearer to his desires. Becoming desperate, he sought and obtained a challenge to a duel, and fell mortally wounded by a ball from his adversary. Two days later he died, having just received a letter from the emperor, saying : —

"DEAR ALEXANDER, Son of Sergius, — If it is the will of Providence that we should never meet again in this world, I counsel you to die like a Christian. Give yourself no anxiety for your wife and children; I will care for them."

Russia cried out with indignation at the news of his death, accusing polite society in round terms of having taken the part of the professional libertine against the husband, — of the French adventurer against their illustrious compatriot; and Lermontof voiced the national anger in some celebrated lines to this effect : —

"Thy last days were poisoned by the vicious ridicule of low detractors; thou hast died thirsting for vengeance, moaning bitterly to see thy most beautiful hopes vanished; none understood the deep emotion of thy last words, and the last sigh of thy dying lips was lost."

But I agree with those who, in spite of this fine elegy, do not regret the premature end of the romantic poet. His life, exuberant, brilliant, fecund, passionate, like that of Byron, could have no more appropriate termination than a pistol-shot. He died before the end of romanticism; his tragic history lent him a halo which lifts his figure above the mists of time. I have seen Victor Hugo and our own Zorilla in their old age, and I was not guilty of wishing them anything but long life and prosperity; but, æsthetically speaking, it seemed to me that both of them had lived forty years too long, and that Alfred de Musset, Espronceda, and Byron were well off in their glorious tombs.

Puchkine belongs undeniably to the great general currents of European literature; only now and then does he manifest the peculiar genius of his country which was so strongly marked in Gogol. But it would be unjust to consider him a mere imitator of foreign romanticists, and some even claim that he always had one foot upon the soil of classicism, taking the phrase in the Helenic sense, as particularly shown in his "Eugene Oneguine," and that, were he to live again, his talents would undergo a transformation and shine forth in the modern novel and the national theatre. Besides being a lyric poet of first rank, Puchkine must also be considered a superb prose writer, having learned from Voltaire a harmony of arrangement, a discreet selection of details, and a concise, clear, and rapid phrasing. His novel, "The Captain's Daughter," is extremely pretty and interesting, at times amusing, or again very touching, and in my opinion preferable in its simplicity to the interminable narratives of Walter Scott. But Puchkine has one remarkable peculiarity, which is, that while he had a keen sympathy with the popular poetry, and was fully sensible of the revelation of it by Gogol, which he applauded with all his heart, yet the author of " Boris Godonof" was so caught in the meshes of romanticism that he never could employ his faculties in poetry of a national character. Puchkine's works have no ethnical value at all. His melancholy is not the despairing sadness of the Russian, but the romantic *morbidezza* expressed often in much the same words by Byron, Espronceda, and de Musset. The phenomenon is common, and easily explained. It lies in the fact that romanticism was always and everywhere prejudicial to the manifestation of nationality, and made itself a nation apart, composed of half-a-dozen persons from every European country. Realism, with its principles — whether tacitly or explicitly accepted — of human verities, heredity, atavism, race and place influences, etc., became a necessity in order that writers might follow their natural instincts and speak in their own mother tongue.

Within the restricted circle of poets who hovered around Puchkine, one deserves especial mention, namely, Lermontof. He is the second lyric poet of Russia, and perhaps embodies the spirit of romanticism even more than Puchkine; he is the real Russian Byron. His life is singularly like that of Puchkine, he having also been banished to the Caucasus, and for the very reason of having written the elegy upon Puchkine's death; like him he was also killed in a duel, but still earlier in life, and before he had reached the plenitude of his powers.

Lermontof became the singer of the Caucasian region. At that time it was really a great favor to send a poet to the mountains, for there he came in contact with things that reclaimed and lifted his fancy, — air, sun, liberty, a wooded and majestic landscape, picturesque and charming peasant-maidens, wild flowers full of new and virginal perfume like the Haydees and Fior d'Alizas sung of by our Western poets. There they forgot the deceits of civilization and the weariness of mind that comes of too much reading; there the brain was refreshed, the nerves calmed, and the moral fibre strengthened. Puchkine, Lermontof, and Tolstoï, each in his own way, have lauded the regenerative virtue of the snow-covered mountains. But Lermontof in particular was full of it, lived in it, and died in it, after his fatal wound at the age of twenty-six, when public opinion had just singled him out as Puchkine's successor. He had drunk deeply of Byron's fountain, and even resembled Byron in his discontent, restlessness, and violent passions, which more than Byron's were tinged with a stripe of malice and pride, so that his enemies used to say that to describe Lucifer he needed only to look at himself in the glass. There is an unbridled freedom, a mocking irony, and at times a deep melancholy at the bottom of his poetic genius; it is inferior to Puchkine's in harmony and completeness, but exceeds it in an almost painful and thrilling intensity; there was more gall in his soul, and therefore more of what has been called subjectivity, even amounting to a fierce egoism. Lermontof is the high-water mark of romanticism, and after his death it necessarily began to ebb; it had exhausted curses, fevers, complaints, and spleens, and now the world of literature was ready for another form of art, wider and more human, and that form was realism.

I am sorry to have to deal in *isms*, but the fault is not mine; we are handling ideas, and language offers no other way. The transition came by means of satire, which is exceptionally fertile in Russia. A genius of wonderful promise arose in Griboiëdof, a keen observer and moralist, who deserves to be mentioned after Puchkine, if only for one comedy which is considered the gem of the Russian stage, and is entitled (freely rendered) "Too Clever by Half." The hero is a misanthropic patriot who sighs for the good old times and abuses the mania for foreign education and imitation. This shows the first impulse of the nation to know and to assert itself in literature as in everything else. Being prohibited by the censor, the play circulated privately in manuscript; every line became a proverb, and the people found their very soul reflected in it. Five years later, when Puchkine was returning from the Caucasus, he met with a company of Georgians who were drawing a dead body in a cart: it was the body of Griboiëdof, who had been assassinated in an insurrection.

Between the decline of the romantic period and the appearance of new forms inspired by a love of the truth, there hovered in other parts of Europe undefined and colorless shapes, sterile efforts and shallow aspirations which never amounted to anything. But not so in Russia. Romanticism vanished quickly, for it was an aristocratic and artificial condition, without root and without fruit conducive to the well-being of a nation which had as yet scarcely entered on life, and which felt itself strong and eager for stimulus and aim, eager to be heard and understood; realism grew up quickly, for the very youth of the nation demanded it. Russia, which until then had trod with docile steps upon the heels of Europe, was at last to take the lead by creating the realistic novel.

She had not to do violence to her own nature to accomplish this. The Russian, little inclined to metaphysics, unless it be the fatalist philosophy of the Hindus, more quick at poetic conceptions than at rational speculations, carries realism in his veins along with scientific positivism; and if any kind of literature be spontaneous in Russia it is the epic, as shown now in fragmentary songs and again in the novels. Before ever they were popular in their own country, Balzac and Zola were admired and understood in Russia.

The two great geniuses of lyric poetry, Puchkine and Lermontof, confirm this theory. Though both perished before the descriptive and observing faculties of their countrymen were matured, they had both instinctively turned to the novel, and perhaps the possible direction of their genius was thus shadowed forth as by accident. Puchkine seems to me endowed with qualities which would have made him a delightful novel-writer. His heroes are clearly and firmly drawn and very attractive; he has a certain healthy joyousness of tone which is quite classic, and a brightness and freedom of coloring that I like; in the short historic narrative he has left us we never see the slightest trace of the lyric poet. As to Lermontof, is it not marvellous that a man who died at the age of twenty-six years should have produced anything like a novel? But he left a sort of autobiography, which is extremely interesting, entitled "A Contemporary Hero," which hero, Petchorine by name, is really the type of the romantic period, exacting, egotistical, at war with himself and everybody else, insatiable for love, yet scorning life, a type that we meet under different forms in many lands; now swallowing poison like De Musset's Rolla, now refusing happiness like Adolfo, now consumed with remorse like Réné, now cocking his pistol like Werther, and always in a bad humor, and to tell the truth always intolerable. "My hero," writes Lermontof, "is the portrait of a generation, not of an individual." And he makes that hero say, "I have a wounded soul, a fancy unappeased, a heart that nothing can ease. Everything becomes less and less to me. I have accustomed myself to suffering and joy alike, and I have neither feelings nor impressions; everything wearies me." But there are many fine pages in the narratives of Lermontof besides these poetical declamations. Perhaps the novel might also have offered him a brilliant future.

The sad fate of the writers during the reign of Nicholas I. is remarkable, when we consider how favorable it was to art in other respects. Alexander Herzen calculated that within thirty years the three most illustrious Russian poets were assassinated or killed in a duel, three lesser ones died in exile, two became insane, two died of want, and one by the hand of the executioner. Alas! and among these dark shadows we discern one especially sad; it is that of Nicholas Gogol, a soul crushed by its own greatness, a victim to the noblest infirmity and the most generous mania that can come upon a man, a martyr to love of country.

III.

RUSSIAN REALISM: GOGOL, ITS FOUNDER.

Gogol was born in 1809; he was of Cossack blood, and first saw the light of this world amid the steppes which he was afterward to describe so vividly. His grandfather, holding the child upon his knee, amused him with stories of Russian heroes and their mighty deeds, not so very long past either, for only two generations lay between Gogol and the Cossack warriors celebrated in the *bilinas*. Sometimes a wandering minstrel sang these for him, accompanying himself on the *bandura*. In this school was his imagination taught. We may imagine the effect upon ourselves of hearing the Romance of the Cid under such circumstances.

When Gogol went to St. Petersburg with the intention of joining the ranks of Russian youth there, though ostensibly to seek employment, he carried a light purse and a glowing fancy. He found that the great city was a desert more arid than the steppes, and even after obtaining an office under the government he endured poverty and loneliness such as no one can describe so well as himself. His position offered him one advantage which was the opportunity of studying the bureaucratic world, and of drawing forth from amid the dust of official papers the material for some of his own best pages. On the expiration of his term of office he was for a while blown about like a dry leaf. He tried the stage but his voice failed him; he tried teaching but found he had no vocation for it. Nor had he any aptitude for scholarship. In the Gymnasium of Niejine his rank among the pupils was only medium; German, mathematics, Latin, and Greek were little in his line; he was an illiterate genius. But in his inmost soul dwelt the conviction that his destiny held great things in store for him. In his struggle with poverty, the remembrance of the hours he had passed at school reading Puchkine and other romantic poets began to urge him to try his fortune at literature. One day he knocked with trembling hand at Puchkine's door; the great poet was still asleep, having spent the night in gambling and dissipation, but on waking, he received the young novice with a cordial welcome, and with his encouragement Gogol published his first work, called "Evenings at the Farm." It met with amazing success; for the first time the public found an author who could give them a true picture of Russian life. Puchkine had hit the mark in advising him to study national scenes and popular customs; and who knows whether perhaps his conscience did not reproach him with shutting his own eyes to his country and the realities she offered him, and stopping his ears against the voice of tradition and the charms of Nature?

Gogol's "Evenings at the Farm" is the echo of his own childhood; in these pages the Russia of the people lives and breathes in landscapes, peasants, rustic customs, dialogues, legends, and superstitions. It is a bright and simple work, not yet marked with the pessimism which later on darkened the author's soul; it has a strong smell of the soil; it is full of dialect and colloquial diminutive and affectionate terms, with now and then a truly poetical passage. Is it not strange that the intellect of a nation sometimes wanders aimlessly through foreign lands seeking from without what lies handier at home, and borrowing from strangers that of which it has a superabundance already? And how sweet is the surprise one feels at finding so beautiful the things which were hidden from our understanding by their very familiarity!

"The Tales of Mirgorod," which followed the "Evenings at the Farm," contain one of the gems of Gogol's writings, the story of "Taras Boulba." Gogol has the quality of the epic poet, though he is generally noted only for his merits as a novelist; but judging from his greatest works, "Taras Boulba" and "Dead Souls," I consider his epic power to be of the first class, and in truth I hold him to be, rather more than a modern novelist, a master poet who has substituted for the lyric poetry brought into favor by romanticism the epic form, which is much more suited to the Russian spirit. He is the first who has caught the inspiration of the *bilinas*, the hero-songs, the Sclavonic poetry created by the people. The novel, it is true, is one manifestation of epic poetry, and in a certain way every novelist is a rhapsodist who recites his canto of the poem of modern times; but there are some descriptive, narrative fictions, which, imbued with a greater amount of the poetic element united to a certain large comprehensive character, more nearly resemble the ancient idea of the epopee; and of this class I may mention "Don Quixote," and perhaps "Faust," as examples. By this I do not mean to place Gogol on the same plane as Goethe and Cervantes; yet I associate them in my mind, and I see in Gogol's books the transition from the lyric to the epic which is to result in the true novel that begins with Turguenief.

All the world is agreed that "Taras Boulba" is a true prose poem, modelled in the Homeric style, the hero of which is a people that long preserved a primitive character and customs. Gogol declared that he merely allowed himself to reproduce the tales of his grandfather, who thus becomes the witness and actor in this Cossack Iliad.

One charming trait in Gogol is his love for the

past and his fidelity to tradition; they have as strong an attraction for him certainly as the seductions of the future, and both are the outcome of the two sublime sentiments which divide every heart,— retrospection and anticipation. Gogol, who is so skilful in sketching idyllic scenes of the tranquil life of country proprietors, clergy, and peasants, is no less skilful in his descriptions of the adventurous existence of the Cossack; sometimes he is so faithful to the simple grandeur of his grandfather's style, that though the action in "Taras Boulba" takes place in recent times, it seems a tale of primeval days.

The story of this novel — I had almost said this poem — unfolds among the Cossacks of the Don and the Dnieper, who were at that time a well-preserved type of the ancient warlike Scythians that worshipped the blood-stained sword. Old Taras Boulba is a wild animal, but a very interesting wild animal; a rude and majestic warrior-like figure cast in Homeric mould. There is, I confess, just a trace of the leaven of romanticism in Taras. Not all in vain had Gogol hidden Puchkine's works under his pillow in school-days; but the whole general tone recalls inevitably the grand naturalism of Homer, to which is added an Oriental coloring, vivid and tragical. Taras Boulba is an Ataman of the Cossacks, who has two young sons, his pride and his hope, studying at the University of Kief. On a declaration of war between the savage Cossack republic and Poland, the old hawk calls his two nestlings and commands them to exchange the book for the sword. One of the sons, bewitched by the charms of a Polish maiden, deserts from the Cossack camp and fights in the ranks of the enemy; he at length falls into the power of his enraged father, who puts him to death in punishment for his treason. After dreadful battles and sieges, starvation and suffering, Taras dies, and with him the glory and the liberty of the Cossacks. Such is the argument of this simple story, which begins in a manner not unlike the Tale of the Cid. The two sons of Taras arrive at their father's house, and the father begins to ridicule their student garb.

"'Do not mock at us, father,' says the elder.

"'Listen to the gentleman! And why should I not mock at you, I should like to know?'

"'Because, even though you are my father, I swear by the living God, I will smite you.'

"'Hi! hi! What? Your father?' cries Taras, receding a step or two.

"'Yes, my own father; for I will take offence from nobody at all.'

"'How shall we fight then, — with fists?' exclaims the father in high glee.

"'However you like.'

"'With fists, then,' answers Taras, squaring off at him. 'Let us see what sort of fellow you are, and what sort of fists you have.'"

And so father and son, instead of embracing after a long absence, begin to pommel one another with naked fists, in the ribs, back, and chest, each advancing and receding in turn.

"'Why, he fights well,' exclaims Taras, stopping to take breath. 'He is a hero,' he adds, readjusting his clothes. 'I had better not have put him to the proof. But he will be a great Cossack! Good! my son, embrace me now.'"

This is like the delight of Diego Lainez in the Spanish Romanceros, when he says, "Your anger appeases my own, and your indignation gives me pleasure."

Could Gogol have been acquainted with the Tale of the Cid and the other Spanish Romanceros? I do not think it too audacious to believe it possible, when we know that this author was a delighted reader of "Don Quixote," and really drew inspiration from it for his greatest work. But let us return to "Taras Boulba." Another admirable passage is on the parting of the mother and sons. The poor wife of Taras is the typical woman of the warlike tribes, a gentle and miserable creature amid a fierce horde of men who are for the most part celibates, — a creature once caressed roughly for a few moments by her harsh husband, and then abandoned, and whose love instincts have concentrated themselves upon the fruits of his early fugitive affection. She sees again her beloved sons who are to spend but one night at home, — for at break of day the father leads them forth to battle, where perhaps at the first shock some Tartar may cut off their heads and hang them by the hair at his saddle-girths. She watches them while they sleep, kept awake herself by hope and fear.

"'Perhaps,' she says to herself, 'when Boulba awakes he will put off his departure one or two days; perhaps he was drunk, and did not think how soon he was taking them away from me.'"

But at dawn her maternal hopes vanish; the old Cossack makes ready to set off.

"When the mother saw her sons leap to horse, she rushed toward the younger, whose face showed some trace of tenderness; she grasped the stirrup and the saddle-girth, and would not let go, and her eyes were wide with agony and despair. Two strong Cossacks seized her with firm but respectful hands, and bore her away to the house. But scarcely had they released her upon the threshold, when she sprang out again quicker than a mountain-goat, which was the more remarkable in a woman of her age; with superhuman effort she held back the horse, gave her son a wild, convulsive embrace, and again was carried away. The young Cossacks rode off in silence, choking their tears for fear of their father; and the father, too, had a queer feeling about his heart, though he took care that it should not be noticed."

In another place I have translated his magnificent description of the steppe, and I should like to quote the admirable paragraphs on starvation, on the killing of Ostap Boulba, and the death of Taras. As an example of the extreme simplicity with which Gogol manages his most dramatic passages and yet obtains an intense and powerful effect, I will give the scene in which Taras takes the life of his son by his own hand, — a scene which Prosper Merimée imitated in his celebrated sketch of "Mateo Falcone."

Andry comes out of the city, which was attacked by the Cossacks.

"At the head of the squadron galloped a horseman, handsomer and haughtier than the others. His black hair floated from beneath his bronze helmet; around his arm was bound a beautifully embroidered scarf. Taras was stupefied on recognizing in him his son Andry. But the latter, inflamed with the ardor of combat, eager to merit the prize which adorned his arm, threw himself forward like a young hound, the handsomest, the fleetest, the strongest of the pack. . . . Old Taras stood a moment, watching Andry as he cut his way by blows to the right and the left, laying the Cossacks about him. At last his patience was exhausted.

"'Do you strike at your own people, you devil's whelp?' he cried.

"Andry, galloping hard away, suddenly felt a strong hand pulling at his bridle-rein. He turned his head and saw Taras before him. He grew pale, like a child caught idling by his master. His ardor cooled as though it had never blazed; he saw only his terrible father, motionless and calm before him.

"'What are you doing?' exclaimed Taras, looking at the young man sharply. Andry could not reply, and his eyes remained fixed upon the ground.

"'How now, my son? Have your Polish friends been of much use to you?' Andry was dumb as before.

"'You commit felony, you barter your religion, you sell your own people. . . . But wait, wait. . . . Get down.' Like an obedient child Andry alighted from his horse, and, more dead than alive, stood before his father.

"'Stand still. Do not move. I gave you life, I will take your life away,' said Taras then; and going back a step he took the musket from his shoulder. Andry was white as wax. He seemed to move his lips and to murmur a name. But it was not his country's name, nor his mother's, nor his brother's; it was the name of the beautiful Polish maiden. Taras fired. As the wheatstalk bends after the stroke of the sickle, Andry bent his head and fell upon the grass without uttering a word. The man who had slain his son stood a long time contemplating the body, beautiful even in death. The young face, so lately glowing with strength and winsome beauty, was still wonderfully comely, and his eyebrows, black and velvety, shaded his pale features.

"'What was lacking to make him a true Cossack?' said Boulba. 'He was tall, his eyebrows were black, he had a brave mien, and his fists were strong and ready to fight. And he has perished, perished without glory, like a cowardly dog.'"

In the opinion of Guizot there is perhaps no true epic poem in the modern age besides "Taras Boulba," in spite of some defects in it and the temptation to compare it with Homer to its disadvantage. But Gogol's glory is not derived solely from his epopee of the Cossacks. His especial merit, or at least his greatest service to the literature of his country, lies in his having been what neither Lermontof nor Puchkine could be; namely, the centre at which romanticism and realism join hands, the medium of a smooth and easy transition from lyric poetry, more or less imported from abroad, and the national novel; the founder of the *natural school*, which was the advance sentinel of modern art.

This tendency is first exhibited in a little sketch inserted in the same volume with Taras Boulba, and entitled "The Small Proprietors of Former

Times," also translated as "Old-fashioned Farmers," or "Old-time Proprietors," — a story of the commonplace, full of keen observations and wrought out in the methods of the great contemporary novelists. About the year 1835, at the height of the romantic period, Gogol gave up his official employment forever, exclaiming, "I am going to be a free Cossack again; I will belong to nobody but myself." He then published a little volume of *Arabesques*, — a collection of disconnected articles, criticisms, and sketches, chiefly interesting because by him. His short stories of this period are the stirrings of his awakening realism; and among them the one most worthy of notice is "The Cloak," which is filled with a strain of sympathy and pity for the poor, the ignorant, the plain, and the dull people, — social zeros, so different from the proud and aristocratic ideal of romanticism, and who owe their title of citizenship in Russian literature to Gogol. The hero of the story is an awkward, half-imbecile little office-clerk, who knows nothing but how to copy, copy, copy; a martyr to bitter cold and poverty, and whose dearest dream is to possess a new cloak, for which he saves and hoards sordidly and untiringly. The very day on which he at last fulfils his desire, some thieves make off with his precious cloak. The police, to whom he carries his complaint, laugh in his face, and the poor fellow falls a victim to the deepest melancholy, and dies of a broken heart shortly after.

"And," says Gogol, "St. Petersburg went on its way without Acacio, son of Acacio, just exactly as though it had never dreamed of his existence. This creature that nobody cared for, nobody loved, nobody took any interest in, — not even the naturalist who sticks a pin through a common fly and studies it attentively under a microscope, — this poor creature disappeared, vanished, went to the other world without anything in particular ever having happened to him in this. . . . But at least once before he died he had welcomed that bright guest, Fortune, whom we all hope to see; to his eyes she appeared under the form of a cloak. And then misfortune fell upon him as suddenly and as darkly as it ever falls upon the great ones of the earth."

"The Cloak" and his celebrated comedy, "The Inspector," also translated as "The Revizor," are the result of his official experiences. Men who have been a good deal tossed about, who have drunk of life's cup of bitterness, who have been bruised by its sharp corners and torn by its thorns, if they have an analytical mind and a magnanimous heart, human kindness and a spark of genius, become the great satirists, great humorists, and great moralists. "The Inspector" is a picture of Russian public customs painted by a master hand; it is a laugh, a fling of derision, at the baseness of a society and a political regimen under which bureaucracy and official formalism can descend to incredible vice and corruption. It seems at first a mere farce, such as is common enough on the Russian or any stage; but the covert strength of the satire is so far-reaching that the "Inspector" is a symbolical and cruel work. The curtain rises at the moment when the officials of a small provincial capital are anxiously awaiting the Inspector, who is about to make them a visit incognito. A traveller comes to the only hotel or inn of the town, and all believe him to be the dreaded governmental attorney. It turns out that the traveller who has given them such a fright is neither more nor less than an insignificant employee from St. Petersburg, — a madcap fellow, who, having run short of money, is obliged to cut his vacation journey short. When he is apprised of a visit from the governor, he thinks he is about to be arrested. What is his astonishment when he finds that, instead of being put in prison, a purse of five hundred rubles is slipped into his hand, and he is conducted with great ceremony to visit hospitals and schools. As soon as he smells the *quid pro quo* he adapts himself to the part, dissimulates, and plays the protector, puts on a majestic and severe demeanor, and after having fooled the whole town and received all sorts of obsequious attentions, he slips out with a full purse. A few minutes afterward the real Inspector appears and the curtain falls.

Gogol frankly confesses that in this comedy he has tried to put together and crystallize all the evil that he saw in the administrative affairs of Russia. The general impression it gave was that of a satire, as he desired; the nation looked at itself in the glass, and was ashamed. "In the midst of my own laughter, which was louder than ever," says Gogol, "the spectator perceived a note of sorrow and anger, and I myself noticed that my laugh was not the same as before, and that it was no longer possible to be as I used to be in my works; the need to amuse myself with innocent fictions was gone with my youth." This is the sincere confession of the humorist whose laughter is full of tears and bitterness.

This rough satire on the government of the autocrat Nicholas, this terrible flagellation of wickedness in high places raised to a venerated national institution, was represented before the court and applauded by it, and the satirical author of it was subjected to no censor but the emperor himself, who read the play in manuscript, burst into roars of laughter over it, and ordered his players to give it without delay; and on the first night Nicholas appeared in his box, and his imperial hands gave the signal for applause. The courtiers could not do otherwise than swallow the pill, but it left a bad taste and a bitter sediment in their hearts, which they treasured up against Gogol for the day of revenge.

On this occasion the terrible autocrat acted with the same exquisite delicacy and truly royal munificence which he had shown toward Puchkine. On allowing Gogol a pension of five thousand rubles, he said to the person who presented the petition, "Do not let your protégé know that this gift is from me; he would feel obliged to write from a government standpoint, and I do not wish him to do that." Several times afterward the Emperor secretly sent him such gifts under cover of his friend Joukowsky the poet, by which means he was able to defray his journeys to Europe.

Without apparent cause Gogol's character became soured about the year 1836; he became a prey to hypochondria, probably, as may be deduced from a passage in one of his letters, on account of the atmosphere of hostility which had hung over him since the publication of "The Inspector." "Everybody is against me," he says, "officials, police, merchants, literary men; they are all gnashing and snapping at my comedy! Nowadays I hate it! Nobody knows what I suffer. I am worn out in body and soul." He determined to leave the country, and he afterward returned to it only occasionally, until he went back at last to languish and die there. Like Turguenief, and not without some truth, he declared that he could see his country, the object of his study, better from a distance; it is the law of the painter, who steps away from his picture to a certain distance in order to study it better. He went from one place to another in Europe, and in Rome he formed a close friendship with the Russian painter Ivanof, who had retired to a Capuchin convent, where he spent twenty years on one picture, "The Apparition of Christ," and left it at last unfinished. Some profess to believe that Gogol was converted to Catholicism, and with his friend devoted himself to a life of asceticism and contemplation of the hereafter, toward which vexed and melancholy souls often feel themselves irresistibly drawn.

Gogol felt a strong desire to deal with the truth, with realities; he longed to write a book that would tell *the whole truth*, which should show Russia as she was, and which should not be hampered by influences that forced him to temporize, attenuate, and weigh his words, — a book in which he might give free vent to his satirical vein, and put his faculties of observation to consummate use. This book, which was to be a *résumé* of life, a *chef d'œuvre*, a lasting monument (the aspiration of every ambitious soul that cannot bear to die and be forgotten), at last became a fixed idea in Gogol's mind; it took complete possession of him, gave him no repose, absorbed his whole life, demanded every effort of his brain, and finally remained unfinished. And yet what he accomplished constitutes the most profoundly human book that has ever been written in Russia; it contains the whole programme of the school initiated by Gogol, and compels us to count the author of it among the descendants of Cervantes. " Don Quixote " was in fact the model for " Dead Souls," which put an end to romanticism, as " Quixote " did to books of chivalry. That none may say that this supposition is dictated by my national pride, I am going to quote literally two paragraphs, one by Gogol himself, the other by Melchior de Voguié, the intelligent French critic whose work on the Russian novel has been so useful to me in these studies.

"Puchkine," says Gogol, "has been urging me for some time to undertake a long and serious work. One day he talked to me of my feeble health, of the frequent attacks which may cause my premature death; he mentioned as an example Cervantes, the author of some short stories of excellent quality, but who would never have held the place he is awarded among the writers of first rank, had he not undertaken his 'Don Quixote.'

And at last he suggested to me a subject of his own invention on which he had thought of making a poem, and said he would tell it to nobody but me. The subject was 'The Dead Souls.' Puchkine also suggested to me the idea of 'The Inspector.'"

"In spite of this frank testimony," adds Voguié, "equally honorable to both friends, I must continue to believe that the true progenitor of 'Dead Souls' was Cervantes himself. On leaving Russia Gogol turned toward Spain, and studied at close quarters the literature of this country, especially 'Don Quixote,' which was always his favorite book. The Spanish humorist held up to him a subject marvellously suited to his plans, the adventures of a hero with a mania which leads him into all regions of society, and who serves as the pretext to show to the spectator a series of pictures, a sort of human magic-lantern. The near relationship of these two works is indicated at all points, — the cogitative, sardonic spirit, the sadness underlying the laughter, and the impossibility of classifying either under any definite literary head. Gogol protested against the application of the word 'novel' to his book, and himself called it a poem, dividing it, not into chapters but into cantos. Poem it cannot be called in any rigorous sense of the term; but classify 'Don Quixote,' and Gogol's masterpiece will fall into the same category."

I read "Dead Souls" before reading Voguié's criticism, and my impression coincided exactly with his. I said to myself, "This book is the nearest like 'Don Quixote' of any that I have ever read." There are important differences — how could it be otherwise? — and even discounting the loss to Gogol by means of translation, a marked inferiority of the

Russian to Cervantes; but they are writers of the same species, and even at the distance of two centuries they bear a likeness to each other. And the intention to take "Don Quixote" as a model is evident, even though Gogol had never set foot in Spain, as some of his compatriots affirm.

"Dead Souls" may be divided into three parts: the first, which was completed and published in 1842; the second, which was incomplete and rudimentary, and cast into the flames by the author in a fit of desperation, but published after his death from notes that had escaped this holocaust; and the third, which never took shape outside the author's mind.

Even the contrast between the heroes of Cervantes and Gogol — the Ingenious Knight Avenger of Wrongs, and the clever rascal who goes from place to place trying to carry out his extravagant schemes — illustrates still more clearly the Cervantesque affiliation of the book. Undoubtedly Gogol purposely chose a contrast, because he wished to embody in the story the wrath he felt at the social state of Russia, more lamentable and hateful even than that of Spain in Cervantes' time. No more profound diatribe than "Dead Souls" has ever been written in Russia, though it is a country where satire has flourished abundantly. Sometimes there is a ray of sunshine, and the poet's tense brows relax with a hearty laugh. In the first chapter is a description of the Russian inns, drawn with no less graceful wit than that of the inns of La Mancha. It is not difficult to go on with the parallel.

In "Dead Souls," as in "Don Quixote," the hero's servants are important personages, and so are their horses, which have become typical under the names of Rocinante and Rucio; the dialogues between the coachman Selifan and his horses remind one of some of the passages between Sancho and his donkey. As in " Don Quixote," the infinite variety of persons and episodes, the physiognomy of the places, the animated succession of incidents, offer a panorama of life. As in "Don Quixote," woman occupies a place in the background; no important love-affair appears in the whole book. Gogol, like Cervantes, shows less dexterity in depicting feminine than masculine types, except in the case of the grotesque, where he also resembles the creator of Maritornes and Teresa Panza. As in "Don Quixote," the best part of the book is the beginning; the inspiration slackens toward the middle, for the reason, probably, that in both the poetic instinct supersedes the prudent forecasting of the idea, and there is in both something of the sublime inconsistency common to geniuses and to the popular muse. And in "Don Quixote," as in "Dead Souls," above the realism of the subject and the vulgarity of many passages there is a sort of ebullient, fantastic life, something supersensual, which carries us along under full sail into the bright world of imagination; something which enlivens the fancy, takes hold upon the mind, and charms the soul; something which makes us better, more humane, more spiritual in effect.

The subject of "Dead Souls" — so strange as

never to be forgotten — gives Gogol a wide range for his pungent satire. Tchitchikof — there's a name, indeed! — an ex-official, having been caught in some nefarious affair, and ruined and dishonored by the discovery, conceives a bright idea as to regaining his fortune. He knows that the serfs, called in Russia by the generic name of *souls*, can be pawned, mortgaged, and sold; and that on the other hand the tax-collector obliges the owners to pay a *per capita* tax for each soul. He remembers also that the census is taken on the Friday before Easter, and in the mean time the lists are not revised, seeing that natural processes compensate for losses by death. But in case of epidemic the owner loses more, yet continues to pay for hands that no longer toil for him; so it occurs to Tchitchikof to travel over the country buying at a discount a number of *dead souls* whose owners will gladly get rid of them, the buyer having only to promise to pay the taxes thereon; then, having provided these dead souls (though to all legal intents still living) with this extraordinary nominal value, he will register them as purchased, take the deed of sale to a bank in St. Petersburg, mortgage them for a good round sum, and with the money thus obtained, buy real live serfs of flesh and blood, and by this clever trick make a fortune. No sooner said than done. The hero gives orders to harness his *britchka*, takes with him his coachman and his lackey, — two delicious characters! — and goes all over Russia, ingratiating himself everywhere, finding out all about the people and the estates, meeting with all sorts of proprietors and functionaries, and falling into many adventures which, if not quite as glorious as those of the Knight of La Mancha, are scarcely less entertaining to read about. And where is such another diatribe on serfdom as this lugubrious burlesque furnishes, or any spectacle so painfully ironical as that of these wretched corpses, who are neither free nor yet within the narrow liberty of the tomb, — these poor bones ridiculed and trafficked for even in the precincts of death?

This remarkable book, which contains a most powerful argument against the inveterate abuses of slavery, unites to its value as a social and humanitarian benefactor that of being the corner-stone of Russian realism, — the realism which, though already perceptible in the prose writings of the romantic poets, appears in Gogol, not as a confused precursory intuition, nor as an instinctive impulse of a national tendency, but as a rational literary plan, well based and firmly established. A few quotations from "Dead Souls," and some passages also from Gogol's Letters, will be enough to prove this.

"Happy is the writer,"[1] he says sarcastically, "who refrains from depicting insipid, disagreeable, unsympathetic characters without any charms whatever, and makes a study of those more distinguished, refined, and exquisite; the writer who has a fine tact in selecting from the vast and muddy stream of humanity, and devoting his attention to a few honorable exceptions to

---

[1] I could take this passage bodily from the translation of "Dead Souls" made by Isabella Hapgood directly from the Russian, but there are some discrepancies in which the Spanish writer seems to be in the right, as in the use of the word *writer* for *reader*. — TR.

the average human nature; who never once lowers the clear, high tone of his lyre; who never puts his melodies to the ignoble use of singing about folk of no importance and low quality; and who, in fact, taking care never to descend to the too commonplace realities of life, soars upward bright and free toward the ethereal regions of his poetic ideal! . . . He soothes and flatters the vanity of men, casting a veil over whatever is base, sombre, and humiliating in human nature. All the world applauds and rejoices as he passes by in his triumphal chariot, and the multitude proclaims him a great poet, a creative genius, a transcendent soul. At the sound of his name young hearts beat wildly, and sweet tears of admiration shine in gentle eyes. . . . Oh, how different is the lot of the unfortunate writer who dares to present in his works a faithful picture of social realities, exactly as they appear to the naked eye! Who bade him pay attention to the muddy whirlpool of small miseries and humiliations, in which life is perforce swallowed up, or take notice of the crowd of vulgar, indifferent, bungling, corrupt characters, that swarm like ants under our feet? If he commit a sin so reprehensible, let him not hope for the applause of his country; let him not expect to be greeted by maidens of sixteen, with heaving bosom and bright, enthusiastic eyes. . . . Nor will he be able to escape the judgment of his contemporaries, a tribunal without delicacy or conscience, which pronounces the works it devours in secret to be disgusting and low, and with feigned repugnance enumerates them among the writings which are hurtful to humanity; a tribunal which cynically imputes to the author the qualities and conditions of the hero whom he describes, allowing him neither heart nor soul, and belittling the sacred flame of talent which is his whole life.

"Contemporary judgment is not yet able or willing to acknowledge that the lens which discloses the habits and movements of the smallest insect is worthy the same estimation as that which reaches to the farthest limits of the firmament. It seems to ignore the fact that it needs a great soul indeed to portray sincerely and accurately the life that is stigmatized by public opinion, to convert clay into precious pearls through the medium of art. Contemporary judgment finds it hard to realize that frank, good-natured laughter may be as full of merit and dignity as a fine outburst of lyric passion. Contemporary judgment pretends ignorance, and bestows only censure and depreciation upon the sincere author, — knows him not, disdains him; and so he is left wretched, abandoned, without sympathy, like the lonely traveller who has no companion but his own indomitable heart.

"I understand you, dear readers; I know very well what you are thinking in your hearts; you curse the means that shows you palpable, naked human misery, and you murmur within yourselves, 'What is the use of such an exhibition? As though we did not already know enough of the absurd and base actions that the world is always full of! These things are annoying, and one sees enough of them without having them set before us in literature. No, no; show us the beautiful, the charming; that which shall lift us above the levels of reality, elevate us, fill us with enthusiasm.' And this is not all. The author exposes himself to the anger of a class of would-be patriots, who, at the least indication of injury to the country's decorum, at the first appearance of a book that dwells on some bitter truths, raise a dreadful outcry. 'Is it well that such things should be brought to light?' they say; 'this description may apply to a good many people we know;

it might be you, or I, or our friend there. And what will foreigners say? It is too bad to allow them to form so poor an opinion of us.' Hypocrites! The motive of their accusations is not patriotism, that noble and beautiful sentiment; it is mean, low calculation, wearing the mask of patriotism. Let us tear off the mask and tread it under foot. Let us call things by their names; it is a sacred duty, and the author is under obligation to tell the truth, the whole truth."

These passages just quoted are sufficiently explicit; but the following, taken from one of Gogol's letters concerning "Dead Souls," is still more so.

"Those who have analyzed my talents as a writer have not been able to discover my chief quality. Only Puchkine noticed it, and he used to say that no author had, so much as I, the gift of showing the reality of the trivialities of life, of describing the petty ways of an insignificant creature, of bringing out and revealing to my readers infinitesimal details which would otherwise pass unnoticed. In fact, there is where my talent lies. The reader revolts against the meanness and baseness of my heroes; when he shuts the book he feels as though he had come up from a stifling cellar into the light of day. They would have forgiven me if I had described some picturesque theatrical knave, but they cannot forgive my vulgarity. The Russians are shocked to see their own insignificance."

"My friend," he writes again, "if you wish to do me the greatest favor that I can expect from a Christian, make a note of every small daily act and fact that you may come across anywhere. What trouble would it be to you to write down every night in a sort of diary such notes as these, — To-day I heard such an opinion expressed, I spoke with such a person, of such a disposition, such a character, of good education or not; he holds his hands thus, or takes his snuff so, — in fact, everything that you see and notice from the greatest to the least?"

What more could the most modern novelist say, — the sort that carries a memorandum-book under his arm and makes sketches, after the fashion of the painters?

Thus we see that a man gifted with epic genius became in 1843, before Zola was dreamt of, and when Edmond de Goncourt was scarcely twenty, the founder of realism, the first prophet of the doctrine not inexactly called by some the doctrine of literary microbes, the poet of social atoms whose evolution at length overturns empires, changes the face of society, and weaves the subtle and elaborate woof of history. I will not go so far as to affirm with some of the critics that this light proceeded from the Orient, and that French realism is an outcome of distant Russian influence; for certainly Balzac had a large influence in his turn upon his Muscovite admirers. But it is undeniable that Gogol did anticipate and feel the road which literature, and indeed all forms of art, were bound to follow in the latter half of the nineteenth century.

Certain critics see, in this doctrine of literary microbes preached by Gogol in word and deed, nothing less than an immense evolution, characteristic of and appropriate to our age. It is the advent of literary democracy, which was perhaps foreseen by the subtle genius of those early novelists who described the beggar, the lame, halt, and blind, thieves and robbers, and creatures of the lowest strata of society; with the difference that to-day, united to this spirit of æsthetic demagogy, there is a shade of Christian charity, compassion, and sympathy for wretchedness and misery which sometimes degenerates, in less virile minds than Gogol's, into an affected sentimentality. George Eliot, that great author and great advocate of Gogol's own theories, and the patroness of realism of humblest degree, speaks in words very like those used by the author of "Taras," of the strength of soul which a writer needs to interest himself in the vulgar commonplaces of life, in daily realities, and in the people around us who seem to have nothing picturesque or extraordinary about them. If there be any who could carry out this rehabilitation of the miserable with charity and tenderness, it would be the Saxon and the Sclav rather than the refined and haughty Latin, and in both these the seed scattered by Gogol has brought forth fruit abundantly. Modern Russian literature is filled with pity and sincere love toward the poorer classes; one might almost term it evangelical unction; at the voice of the poet (I cannot refuse this title to the author of "Taras") Russia's heart softened, her tears fell, and her compassion, like a caressing wave, swept over the toiling *mujik*, the ill-clad government clerk, the ragged, ignorant beggar, the political convict in the grasp of the police, and even the criminal, the vulgar assassin with shaven head, mangled shoulders, blood-stained hands, and manacled wrists. And more; their pity extends even to the dumb beasts, and the death of a horse mentioned by one great Russian novelist is more touching than that of any emperor.

Gogol is the real ancestor of the Russian novel; he contained the germs of all the tendencies developed in the generation that came after him; in him even Turguenief the poet and artist, Tolstoï the philosopher, and Dostoiëwsky the visionary, found inspiration. There are writers who seem possessed of the exalted privilege of uniting and accumulating all the characteristics of their race and country; their brain is like a cave filled with wonderful stalactites formed by the deposits of ages and events. Gogol is one of these. The peculiarities of the Russian soul, the melancholy dreaminess, the satire, the suppressed and resigned soul-forces, are all seen in him for the first time.

To quote from " Dead Souls " would be little satisfaction. One must read it to understand the deep impression it made in Russia. After looking it through, Puchkine exclaimed, " How low is our country fallen!" and the people, much against their will, finally acknowledged the same conviction. After a hard fight with the censors, the work of art came off at last victorious; it captured all classes of minds, and became, like " Don Quixote," the talk of every drawing-room, the joke of every meeting-place, and a proverb everywhere. The serfs were now virtually set free by force of the opinion created, and the whole nation saw and knew itself in this æsthetic revelation.

But the man who dares to make such a revelation must pay for his temerity with his life. Gogol returned from Rome intent upon the completion of the fatal book; but his nerves, which were almost worn out, failed him utterly at times, his soul overflowed with bitterness and gall, and at last in a fit of rage and desperation he burned the manuscript of the Second Part, together with his whole library. His darkened mind was haunted by the question in Hamlet's monologue, the problem concerning "that bourn from which no traveller returns;" his meditations took a deeply religious hue, and his last work, "Letters to my Friends," is a collection of edifying epistles, urging the necessity of the consideration of the hereafter. To these exhortations he added one on Sclavophile nationalism, exaggerated by a fanatical devotion; and in the same breath he heralds the spirit of the Gospels and anathematizes the theories imported from the Occident, and declares that he has given up writing for the sake of dedicating his time to self-introspection and the service of his neighbor, and that henceforth he recognizes nothing but his country and his God. The public was exasperated; it was Gogol's fate to rouse the tiger. Who ever heard of a satirist turning Church father? It began to be whispered that Gogol had become a devotee of mysticism; and it is quite true that on his return from a pilgrimage to Jerusalem he lived miserably, giving all he had to the poor. He was hypochondriac and misanthropic, excepting when with children, whose innocent ways brought back traces of his former good-nature. His death is laid to two different causes. The general story is that during the Revolution of 1848 he lost what little intelligence remained to him, under the conviction that there was no remedy for his country's woes; and at last, weighed down by an incurable melancholy and despair, and terrified by visions of universal destruction and other tremendous catastrophes, he fell on his knees and fasted for a whole day before the holy pictures that hung at the head of his bed, and was found there dead. Recent writers modify this statement, and claim to know on good authority that Gogol died of a typhoid fever, which, with his chronic infirmities, was a fatal complication. Whatever may have been the illness which took him out of the world, it is certain that the part of Gogol most diseased was his soul, and his sickness was a too intense love of country, which could not see with indifferent optimism the ills of the present or the menace of the future. Gogol had no heart-burdens except the suffering he endured for the masses; he was unmarried, and was never known to have any passion but a love of country exaggerated to a dementia.

It is a strange thing that Gogol — the sincere reactionist, the admirer of absolutism and of autocracy, the Pan-Sclavophile, the habitual enemy of Western paganism and liberal theories — should have been the one to throw Russian letters into their present mad whirl, into the path of nihilism and into the currents of revolution, — a course which he seems to have described once in allegory, in one of the most admirable pages of "Dead Souls," where he compares Russia to a *troïka*. I will quote it, and so take my farewell of this Russian Cervantes: —

"Rapidity of motion [in travel] is like an unknown force, a hidden power which seizes us and carries us on its wings; we skim through the air, we fly, and everything else flies too; the verst-stones fly; the tradesmen's carts fly past on one side and the other; forests with dark patches of pines rush by, and the noise of destroying axes and the cawing of hungry crows; the road flies by and is lost in the distance where we can distinguish neither object nor form nor color, unless it be a bit of the sky or the moon continually crossed by patches of flying cloud. O troïka, troïka, bird-troïka! There is no need to ask who invented thee! Thou couldst not have been conceived save in the breast of a quick, active people, in the midst of a gigantic territory that covers half the globe, and where nobody dares count the verst-stones on the roads for fear of vertigo! Thou art not graceful in thy form, O telega, rustic britchka, kibitka, thou carriage for all roads in winter or summer! No, thou art not an object of art made to please the eye; dry wood, a hatchet, a chisel, a clever arm, — with these thou art set up; there is not a peasant in Yaroslaf that knows not how to construct thee. Now the troïka is harnessed. And where is the man? What man? The driver? Aha! it is this same peasant! Very well, let him put on his boots and get up on his seat. Did you say his boots? This is no German postilion; he needs no boots nor any foot-gear at all. All that he needs is mittens for his hands and a beard on his chin! See him balancing himself; hear him sing. Now he pulls away like a whirlwind; the wheels seem a smooth circle from centre to circumference, and the tires are invisible; the ground rushes to meet the clattering hoofs; the foot-traveller leaps to one side with a cry of fright, then stops and opens his mouth in astonishment; but the vehicle has passed, and on it flies, on it flies, and far away a little whirl of dust rises, spreads out, divides, and disappears in gauzy patches, falling gently upon the sides of the road. It is all gone; nothing remains of it.

"Thou art like the troïka, O Russia, my beloved country! Dost thou not feel thyself carried onward toward the unknown like this impetuous bird which nobody can overtake? The road is invisible under thy feet, the bridges echo and groan, and thou leavest everything behind thee in the distance. Men stop and gaze surprised at this celestial portent. Is it the lightning? Is it the thunderbolt from heaven itself? What causes this movement of universal terror? What mysterious and incomprehensible force spurs on thy steeds? They are Russian steeds, good steeds. Doth the whirlwind sometimes nestle in their manes? The signal is given: three bronze breasts expand; twelve ready feet start with simultaneous impetus, their light hoofs scarce striking the ground; three horses are changed before our very eyes into three parallel lines which fly like a streak through the tremulous air. The troïka flies, sails, bright as a spirit of God. O Russia, Russia! whither goest thou? Answer! But there is no response; the bell clangs with a supernatural tone; the air, beaten and lashed, whistles and whirls, and rushes off in wide currents; the troïka cuts them all on the wing, and nations, monarchies, and empires stand aside and let her pass."

Book IV.

MODERN RUSSIAN REALISM.

I.

TURGUENIEF, POET AND ARTIST.

In reviewing the development of the School of Realists founded by Nicholas Gogol, I shall begin with the one among his followers and descendants who is not merely the first in chronological order, but the most intelligible and sympathetic of the Russian novelists, Ivan Turguenief.

The name of Turguenief has long been well known in Russia. In 1854, before the novelist made his appearance, Humboldt said to a member of this family, "The name you bear commands the highest respect and esteem in this country." Alexander Turguenief was a savant, and the originator of a new style of historiography, in which he revealed traces of the communicative and cosmopolitan instincts that distinguish his nephew beyond other novelists of his country, for he — the uncle — courted acquaintance with many of the most eminent men of Europe, among them Walter Scott. Another member of the family, Nicholaï Turguenief, was a statesman who found himself obliged to reside in foreign lands on account of political vicissitudes; he had the honor of preceding his nephew Ivan in the advocacy of serf-emancipation.

Ivan was the son of a country gentleman, and his real education began among the heathery hills and in the company of indefatigable hunters, whose stories, colored by the blaze of the camp-fire, were transcribed afterward by Ivan's wonderful pen. His intellect was awakened and formed in Berlin, where he ranged through the philosophies of Kant and Hegel, and, as he expresses it, threw himself head-first into the ocean of German thought and came out purified and regenerated for the rest of his life. Is it not wonderful, — the power of this German philosophy, which, though it seems but a chilly and lugubrious labyrinth, gives a new temper to a mind of fine and artistic quality, like the Toledo blade thrust into the cold bath, or Achilles after washing in the waters of the Styx? As scholasticism gave a strange power to the poetry of Dante, so German metaphysics seems to give wings to the imagination in our times. Those artist writers (like Zola, for example) who have not wandered through this dark forest seem to lack a certain tension in their mental vigor, a certain tone in their artistic spectrum!

Russian youth, about the year 1838, had their Mecca in the Faculty of Philosophy at Berlin, of which Hegel held one chair; and there the future celebrities of Russia were wont to meet. On leaving that radiant atmosphere of ideas and returning to his country home in Russia, Turguenief was overcome by the inevitable melancholy which attacks the man who leaves civilization behind with its intellectual brightness and activity, and enters a land where, according to the words of the hero of " Virgin Soil," "everything sleeps but the wine-shop." This feeling of nostalgia the novelist has analyzed with a master hand in the pages of " The Nobles' Nest."[1]

Hungry for wider horizons and for a literary life and atmosphere, Turguenief went to St. Petersburg. All the intellect of the time was grouped about Bielinsky, who was a rare critic, and its sentiments were voiced by a periodical called the "Contemporary." Bielinsky, who had adopted the pessimist theory that Russian art could never exist until there was political emancipation, was obliged to acknowledge the indisputable worth of Turguenief's first efforts, and encouraged him to publish some excellent sketches in a collection entitled " Papers of a Sportsman." Contrary to Bielinsky's prediction, Turguenief's success was the greater because, with that exquisite artistic intuition which he alone of all Russian writers possesses, he preached no moral and taught no lesson in it, which was the fashion or rather the pest of the novel in those days.

Turguenief again went abroad soon after and spent some time in Paris, where he finished the " Diary "

---

[1] This work is better known to American readers in a translation entitled " Lisa." — TR.

and wrote "The Nobles' Nest." On his return to Russia he wrote a clever criticism on the "Dead Souls," of Gogol, whom he ventured to call a great man; and this called down upon his head the ire of the police and banishment to his estates, which punishment was not reprieved until the death of Nicholas and the war of the Crimea changed the aspect of everything in Russia.

Notwithstanding the unjustifiable severity with which he was treated on this occasion, Turguenief cherished no grievance or thought of revenge in his heart. It is one of the most beautiful and attractive traits in the amiable character of this man, that he could always preserve his serenity of soul in the midst of the distractions occasioned him by two equally violent parties each equally determined to embitter his life if he did not consent to embrace it. He stood in the gulf that separates the two halves of Russia, yet he maintained that contemplative and thoughtful attitude which Victor Hugo ascribes to all true thinkers and poets. Urged by family traditions and by the natural equilibrium of his mind to give the preference (in comparing Russia with the rest of Europe) to Western civilization, he protested, with the courage born of conviction, against the blind vanity of the so-called National Party of Moscow, which, while it demanded the liberation of the serfs, was determined to create a new national condition which should be wholly Sclavonic, and would tread under foot every vestige of foreign culture. With equal vigor, but with a fine tact and nothing of effeminacy or æsthetic repugnance, he protested also against the vandalism of the nihilists, whose propositions were set forth in a clever caricature in a satirical paper shortly after the explosion in the Winter Palace at St. Petersburg. It represented the meeting of two nihilists amid a heap of ruins. One asks, " Is everything gone up? " " No," replies the other, " the planet still exists." " Blow it to pieces, then ! " exclaims the first. Yet Turgueníef, who was by no means what we should call a conservative, seeing that he lent his aid to the emancipation of the serfs, was far from approving the new revolutionary barbarism.

Those of Turgueníef's works which are best known and most discussed are consequently those which attack the ignominy of serfdom or the threats of revolutionary terror. In the first category may be mentioned " The Diary of a Hunter " and most of his exquisite short stories ; in the second, " Fathers and Sons," a view of speculative nihilism, " Virgin Soil," the active side of the same, and " Smoke," a harsh satire on the exclusiveness and fanaticism of the Nationals, which cost him his popularity and made him innumerable enemies. I will speak more at length of each of these, and it is in no sense a digression from Turgueníef's biography to do so ; for the life of this amiable dreamer and delicate poet is to be found in his books, and in the trials which he endured on their account.

The first lengthy novel of Turgueníef is " Demetrius Rudine," a type which might have served as the model for Alphonse Daudet's "Numa Roumestan," a study of one of those complex characters, endowed with great aspirations and apparently rich faculties, but who lack force of will, and have no definite aim or career in view. "The Nobles' Nest" is to the rest of Turguenief's works what the hour of supreme and tenderest emotion that even the hardest hearts must bow to some time is to human life as a whole; in none of his works, save perhaps in "Living Relics," has Turguenief shown more depth of sentiment. The latter is a tear of compassion crystallized and set in gold; the former is a tragedy of happiness held before the eyes and then lost sight of, like the blue sky seen through a rent in the clouds and then covered over with a leaden and interminable veil. The hero is a Russian gentleman or small proprietary nobleman, named Lawretsky, who, deceived and betrayed by his wife, returns to his patrimonial estates, there to hide his dejection and loneliness. Amid these scenes of honest, simple provincial life he meets with a cousin who is young, beautiful, and open-hearted, and who captures his heart. There is a rumor that his wife has died, and a hope of future happiness begins to revive in him; but the aforesaid deceased lady resuscitates, and makes her appearance, demanding with hypocritical humility her place beneath the conjugal roof, and the other poor girl retires to a convent. It is almost a sacrilege to extract the bare plot of the story in this way, for it is thus made to seem a mere vulgar complication, feeble and colorless. But the charm lies in the manner of presenting this simple drama; the novelist seems to hold a glass before our eyes through which we see the palpitations of these bruised and suffering hearts. The background is worthy of the figures on it. The description of provincial customs, the country, and the last chapter especially, are the perfection of art in the way of novel-writing. It is said that "The Nobles' Nest" produced in Russia an effect comparable only to that of "Paul and Virginia" in France.

Then came the great change in Russia: serfdom was no more! and Turguenief, leaving these touching love-stories, threw himself into the new turmoil, and gave himself up to the study of the struggle between the new state of society and the old, which resulted in the novel, "Fathers and Sons." This book contains the pictures of two generations, and each one, says Merimée, shrewdly, found the portrait of the other well drawn, but called Heaven to witness that that of himself was a caricature; and the cry of the fathers was exceeded by that of the sons, personified in the character of the positivist, Bazarof.

Two old country gentlefolk, a physician and his wife, represent the elder generation, the society of yesterday, and two students the society and generation of to-day. Bazarof is the leader, the ruling spirit of the two latter; the novelist has given him so much vivacity that we seem to hear him, to see his long, withered face, his broad brows, his great greenish eyes, and the prominent bulges on his heavy skull. I have seen such types as this many a time in the streets and alleys of the Latin Quarter, which is the lurking-place of Russian refugees in Paris, and I have said to myself, "There goes a Bazarof, exiled and half dead with hunger, and yet perhaps more eager to set off a few pounds of dynamite under the Grand Opera-House than to breakfast!"

Bazarof, however, is not yet the nihilist who wishes to make a political system out of robbery and assassination, and to defend his theory in learned treatises; he is a young fellow smarting and burning under the contemplation of his country's sad state, and whom the knowledge got by his studies in medicine, natural sciences, and German materialist dogmas has made the bitterest and most intolerable of mortals, throwing away his gifts of intellect and his heart's best and most generous impulses. By reason of his energy of character and intellectual force, he takes the lead over his companion Arcadio, an enthusiastic and unsophisticated boy; and the novel begins with the return of the latter to his father's country-house in company with his adored leader. The two generations then find themselves face to face, two atheistical and demagogic young students, and Arcadio's father and uncle, conservative and ceremonious old men; the shock is immediate and terrible. Bazarof, with his mania for dissecting frogs, his negligent dress, his harsh and dogmatic replies, his coarse frankness, and his odor of drugs and cheap tobacco, inspires antipathy from the first moment, and he is himself made more captious than usual by the appearance of the uncle, Paul, an elegant and distinguished-looking man, who preserves the traditions of French culture, dresses with the utmost care, has a taste for all that is refined and poetical, and wears such finger-nails as, says Bazarof, "would be worth sending to the Exposition." The contrast is as lively as it is curious; every motion, every breath, produces conflict and augments the discord. Arcadio, under his friend's influence, finds a thousand ways to annoy his elders; he sees his father reading a volume of Puchkine, and snatches it out of his hands, giving him instead the ninth edition of "Force and Matter." And after all the poor boy really cannot follow the hard, harsh ideas of Bazarof; but he is so completely under the latter's control, and looks upon him with so much respect and awe, and stands in such fear of his ridicule, that he hides his most innocent and natural sentiments as though they were sinful, and dares not even confess the pleasure he feels at sight of the country and his native village.

"What sort of fellow is your friend Bazarof?" Arcadio's father and uncle inquire of him.

"He is a nihilist," is the response.

"That word must come from the Latin *nihil*," says the father, "and must mean a man that acknowledges and respects nothing."

"It means a man who looks at everything from a critical point of view," says Arcadio, proudly.

Criticism, pitiless analysis, barren and overwhelming, — this is an epitome of Bazarof, the spirit of absolute negation, the contemporary Mephistopheles who begins by taking himself off to the Inferno.

The punishment falls in the right place. Consistently with his physiological theories, Bazarof denies the existence of love, calls it a mere natural instinct, and women *females;* but scarcely does he find himself in contact with a beautiful, interesting, clever woman — somewhat of a coquette too, perhaps — than he falls into her net like a clumsy idealogue that he is, and suffers and curses his fate like the most ardent romanticist. Quite as curious as the antithesis of the two generations in the house of Arcadio's aristocratic father, is the contrast shown in that of the more humble village physician, the father of Bazarof, who is an altogether pathetic personage. He, too, is possessed of a certain pedantic and antiquated culture, and an excellent, kind heart; he adores his son, thinks him a demi-god, and yet cannot by any means understand him. Arcadio's father, on hearing an exposition of the new theories, shrugs his shoulders and exclaims, "You turn everything inside out nowadays. God give you health and a general's position!" The physician, quite nonplussed, murmurs sadly, "I confess that I idolize my son, but I dare not tell him so, for he would be displeased;" and he adds with ridiculous pathos, "What comforts me most is to think that some day men will read in the biography of my son these lines: 'He was the son of an obscure regiment physician who nevertheless had the wisdom to discern his talents from the first, and spared no pains to give him an excellent education.' Here the voice of the old man died away," says the writer. Such details bespeak the great poet. Again when Bazarof is seized with typhus fever and dies, it is not his fate which affects us, but the grief of his old father and mother, who believe that one light of their country has been put out, and that they have lost the best treasure of their uncontaminated and tender old hearts. The death of this atheist makes an admirable page. When, as he is losing consciousness, extreme unction is administered to him, the shudder of horror that passes over his face at sight of the priest in his robes, the smoking incense, the candles burning before the images, is communicated to our own souls.

From 1860 Turguenief remained in France, bound by ties that shaped his course of life. He enjoyed there a reputation not inferior to that which he possessed in his own country; his works were all translated, and his soul was soothed by an almost fraternal intimacy with the greatest French writers, notably Gustave Flaubert and George Sand; and yet his thoughts were never absent from his far-away fatherland, and as a reproof to his fruitless longings he wrote "Smoke," which put the capital of Russia almost in revolt. But Turguenief was no bilious satirist after the style of Gogol, much less a habitual vilifier of existing classes and institutions like Tchedrine; on the contrary, he had a keen observation like Alphonse Daudet, and the sweeping artist-glance which takes in the moral weaknesses as well as physical deformities. The scene of "Smoke" is laid in Baden-Baden, the resort of rich people who go there to enjoy themselves, to gossip, to intrigue, and to throw themselves aimlessly into the maelstrom of frivolous and idle life. The Russian world passes rapidly before our eyes, and last of all the hero, weary and blasé, who with bitter words compares his country to the thin, feathery smoke that rises in the distance. Everything in Russia is smoke, — smoke, and nothing more !

Turguenief was one of those who loved his country well enough to tell her the truth, and to warn her — in an indirect and artistic manner, of course — persistently and incessantly. His was the jealous love of the master for the favorite pupil, of the confessor for the soul under his guidance, of the ardent patriot for his too backward and unambitious nation. Turguenief compared himself, away from his country, to a dead fish kept sound in the snow, but spoiling in time of thaw. He said that in a strange land one lives isolated, without any real props or profound relation to anything whatever, and that he felt his own creative faculties decay for lack of inspiration from his native air; he complained of feeling the chill of old age upon him, and an incurable vacuity of soul. While he thus pined with homesickness, in Russia his books wrought a wholesome change in criticism; the new generation turned its back upon him, and after a general scandal followed an oblivious silence, of the two perhaps the harder to bear.

In 1876 the novel "Virgin Soil" appeared, first in French in the columns of "Le Temps," and then in Russian. It dealt with the same ideas as "Fathers and Sons," save that the nihilism described in it was of the active rather than the speculative sort. It was said at the time that as Turguenief had been fifteen years away from his own country, he was not capable of seeing the nihilist world in its true aspect, a thing to be felt rather than seen, difficult enough to describe near at hand, and much more difficult at a distance; but one must not expect of the novelist what would be impossible even to the political student. To us who are not too learned in revolutionary mysteries, Turguenief's novel is delightful. I believe that there is more or less of political warmth in the judgments expressed upon this "Virgin Soil," and that if the book errs in any particular, it is on the side of the truthfulness of its representative and symbolic qualities. Otherwise, how explain the fact that certain nihilists thought themselves personally portrayed in the character of the hero, or that Turguenief was accused of having received notices and information provided by the police? Yet it seems to me that this book, which gave such offence to the nihilists, shows a lively sympathy with them. All the revolutionary characters are grand, interesting, sincere, and poetic; on the other hand, the official world is made up of egoists, hypocrites, knaves, and fools. In reality, "Virgin Soil," like all the other writings of Turguenief, is the product of a gentle and serene mind, independent of political bias, although both his artistic and his Sclavonic nature weigh the balance in favor of the visionaries who represent the spirit rather than the letter.

"Virgin Soil" was the last of Turguenief's long novels. Another Russian novelist, Isaac Paulowsky, who knew him intimately, has given us some curious information concerning one he had in project, and which he believed would be found among his papers; but it has not yet come to light, and there remains only to speak of his short stories. Perhaps his best claim to reputation and glory rests upon these admirable sketches; and it is Zola's opinion that Turguenief depreciated and wasted his proper talent when he left off making these fine cameo-like studies. Perhaps this is true, as it is certainly undeniable that Turguenief had a master touch in delicate work of this sort, and it suited his intensity of sentiment, his graceful style, and his skill in shading, which distinguish him above his contemporaries. Of his short stories, his episodes of Russian life, I know not which to select; they are filigree and jewels, wrought by the Benvenuto of his trade; brass is gold in his hands, and his chisel excels at every point. But I must mention a few of the most important.

"The Knight of the Steppes," in which the horse tells the story of the love and disappointment which leads his master to despair and suicide, is one of my favorites. The hero resembles Taras Bulba, perhaps, in his savage grandeur; he is a remnant of Asiatic times, brave, proud, generous, uncultured; ruined, thirsting for battle, and perhaps for pillage, bloodshed, and violence.

Beside this I would put the first one in the collection translated and published under the title of "Strange Stories." It is a sketch of mysticism and religious mania peculiar, though not too common, to the Russian temperament. Sophia, a young girl at a ball, while dancing the mazurka with a stranger, speaks to him seriously concerning miracles, ghosts, the immortality of the soul, and the theory of Quietism, and manifests a wish to mortify and subdue her nature and taste martyrdom; next day she carries out her desires by running away, — not with her partner in the dance, but with a demented fanatic, a man of the lowest condition, with whom she lives in chastity, and to whose infirmities she ministers like a mother, and serves him like a slave. Such a picture could only have been conceived in a land that cradled the heroine of "The Threshold," and many another enthusiastic nihilist girl who was ready to lay down her life for her ideals.

The whole volume of "Strange Stories" fascinates us with a superstitious horror. Elias Teglevo, the hero of one of the best of these tales, although a pronounced sceptic, yet believes in the influence of his star, thinks he is predestined to a tragic death, and under this persuasion works himself into a state of mind and body that becomes a hallucination strong enough to lead to suicide, in obedience to what he considers a supernatural mandate. In another tale, "King Lear of the Steppes," the gigantic Karlof has a presentiment of his death on seeing a black colt in his dreams. The great artist reproduced the souls of his characters with laudable fidelity. If supernatural terror is a real and genuine sentiment, the novel should not overlook it in its delineations of the truth.

But perhaps the jewel of Turguenief's narratives is that entitled "Living Relics." In this simple story he excels himself. The novel has no plot, and is nothing more than a silver lake which reflects a beautiful soul, calm and clear as the moon; and the crippled form of Lukeria is only the pretext for the detention of such a soul in this world. Who has not sometimes entered a convent church on leaving a ball-room, — in the early morning hours of Ash-Wednesday, for instance? The ears still echo the voluptuous and stirring sounds of the military band; one is ready to drop with fatigue, dizziness, glare of lights, and the unseasonable hour. But the church is dark and empty; the nuns in the choir are chanting the psalms; above the altar flickers a dim light, by whose aid one discerns a picture or a statue, though at a distance one cannot make out details of face or figure, only an expression of vague sweetness and mysterious peace. After a moment's contemplation of it, the body forgets its weariness and the soul is rocked in tranquillity. Read some novel of the world's life, and then read "Living Relics": it is like going from the ball-room to the chapel of a convent.

This faculty of putting the reader in contact with the invisible world is not the talent of Turguenief exclusively, for all the great Russian novelists possess it in some degree; but Turguenief uses it with such exquisite tact and poetic charm that he seems to look serenely upon the strange psychical phenomenon he has produced in the soul of the reader, who is roused to a state of excitement that reflects the vision evoked by the artist's words. Other instances of his power in this direction are "The Dog," "Apparitions," and "Clara Militch," a confession from beyond the tomb.

The last page written by Turguenief bore the title of "Despair,"—the voice of the Russian soul whose depths he had searched for forty years, says Voguié. He was then laboring under an incurable disease, cancer of the brain, which, after causing him horrible sufferings, ended his life. But though worn-out, dying, and stupefied by doses of opium and injections of morphine, his artistic faculties died hard; and he related his dreams and hallucinations with wonderful vividness, only regretting his lack of strength to put them on paper. It is said that some of these feverish visions are preserved in his "Prose Poems," which are examples of the adaptability of Turguenief's talent to miniature, condensed, bird's-eye pictures. Like Meissonier, Turguenief saw the light upon small surfaces, enhanced rather than lessened in brilliancy. I will translate one of these prose-poems, so that the reader may see how Turguenief cuts his medallions. This one is entitled "Macha":—

"When I was living in St. Petersburg, some time ago, I was in the habit of entering into conversation with the sleigh-driver, whenever I hired one.

"I particularly liked to chat with those who were engaged at night,—poor peasants from the surrounding country, who came to town with their old-fashioned rattling vehicles, besmeared with yellow mud and drawn by one poor horse, to earn enough for bread and taxes.

"On a certain day I called one of these to me. He was a lad of perhaps twenty years, strong and robust-looking, with blue eyes and red cheeks. Ringlets of reddish hair escaped from under his patched cap, which was pressed down over his eyebrows, and a torn caftan, too small for him, barely covered his broad shoulders.

"It seemed to me that this handsome, beardless young driver's face was sad and gloomy; we fell to chatting, and I noticed that his voice had a sorrowful tone.

"'Why so sad, brother?' I asked. 'Are you in trouble?'

"At first he did not reply.

"'Yes, barino, I am in trouble,' he said at last, — 'a trouble so great that there is no other like it, — my wife is dead.'

"'By this I judge that you were very fond of her.'

"The lad, without turning, nodded his head.

"'Barino, I loved her. It is now eight months, and I cannot get my thoughts away from her. There is something gnawing here at my heart continually. I do not understand why she died; she was young and healthy. In twenty-four hours she was carried off by the cholera.'

"'And was she good?'

"'Ah, barino!' the poor fellow sighed deeply, 'we were such good friends! And she died while I was away. As soon as I heard up here that — that they had buried her — that very moment I started on foot to my village, to my home. I arrived; it was past midnight. I entered my *isba;* I stood still in the middle of it, and called very low, "Macha, oh Macha!" No answer, — nothing but the chirp of a cricket in a corner. Then I burst into tears; I sat down on the ground and beat it with my hand, saying, "O thou greedy earth, thou hast swallowed her! thou must swallow me too! Macha, oh Macha!" I repeated hoarsely.'

"Without loosening his hold on the reins, he caught a falling tear on his leather glove, shook it off at one side, shrugged his shoulders, and said not another word.

"On alighting from the sleigh I gave him a good fee; he bowed himself to the ground before me, taking off his cap with both hands, turned again to his sleigh, and started off at a weary trot down the frozen and deserted street, which was fast filling with a cold, gray, January fog."

Is it a mistake to say that in this commonplace little episode there is more of poetry than in many elegies and innumerable sonnets? I believe there is no Spanish or French writer who would know how to gather up and thread like a pearl the tear of a common coachman. There is something in the Latin character that makes us hard toward the lower classes and the vulgar professions.

Like many another author, Turguenief was not a good judge of his own merits, and gave great importance to his longer novels in preference to his admirable shorter ones, in which he scarcely has a rival. He had great expectations of "Smoke," and the dislike it met with in Russia surprised him painfully. So keen was his disappointment that he determined to write no more original novels, but devote himself to his early cherished plan of translating "Don Quixote." He also suffered in one way like most souls who hang upon the lips of public opinion, — the slightest censure hurt him like a mortal wound.

The cordial and enthusiastic reception which, in spite of past indignation, he was accorded in Russia in 1878, and the homage and attentions of the students of Moscow, renewed his courage and reanimated his soul. . . . But his strong constitution failed him at last, and his physical and mental abilities weakened. "The saddest thing that has happened to me," he said to Paulowsky, "is that I take no more pleasure in my work. I used to love literary labor, as one loves to caress a woman; now I detest it. I have many plans in my head, but I can do nothing at all with them." But after all, what posthumous work of Turguenief would bear with a deeper meaning on his literary life than the admirable words of his letter to Count Leon Tolstoï: —

"It is time I wrote you; for, be it said without the least exaggeration, I have been, I am, on my death-bed. I have no false hopes. I know there is no cure. Let this serve to tell you that I rejoice to have been your contemporary, and to make of you one supreme last request to which you must not turn a deaf ear. Go back, dear friend, to your literary work. The gift you have is from above, whence comes every good gift we possess. How happy I should be if I could believe that my entreaty would have the effect I desire!

"As for myself, I am a drowning man. The physicians have not come to any conclusion about my disease. They say it may be gouty neuralgia of the stomach. I cannot walk, nor eat, nor sleep; but it would be tiresome to enter into details. My friend, great and beloved writer in Russian lands, hear my prayer. With these few lines receive a warm embrace for yourself, your wife, and all your family. I can write no more. I am tired."

This pathetic document contains the essence of the writer's life, the synthesis of a soul that loved art above all things else, and believed that of the three divine attributes, truth, goodness, and beauty, the last is the one especially revealed to the artist, and the one it is his especial duty to show forth; and that he who allows his sacred flame to go out, commits a sin which is great in proportion to his talents, and a sin incalculable when commensurate with the genius of Tolstoï.

Turguenief is the supreme type of the artist, for he had the tranquillity and equipoise of soul, the bright serenity, and the æsthetic sensibility which should distinguish it. According to able critics, such as Taine, Turguenief was one of the most artistic natures that has been born among men since classic times. Those who can read his works in the Russian sing marvellous praises of his style, and even through the haze of translation we are caught by its charms. Let me quote some lines of Melchior de Voguié:

"Turguenief's periods flow on with a voluptuous languor, like the broad expanse of the Russian rivers beneath the shadows of the trees athwart them, slipping melodiously between the reeds and rushes, laden with floating blossoms and fallen bird's-nests, perfumed by wandering odors, reflecting sky and landscape, or suddenly darkened by a lowering cloud. It catches all, and gives each a place; and its melody is blended with the hum of bees, the cawing of the crows, and the sighing of the breeze. The most fugitive sounds of Nature's great organ he can echo in the infinite variety of the tones of the Russian speech, — flexible and comprehensive epithets, words strung together to please a poet's fancy, and bold popular sallies."

Such is the effect produced by a thorough reading of Turguenief's works; it is a symphony, a sweet and solemn music like the sounds of the forest. Turguenief is, without exaggeration, the best word-painter of landscape that ever wrote. His descriptions are neither very long nor very highly colored; there is a charming sobriety about them that reminds one of the saving strokes with which the skilful painter puts life into his trees and skies without stopping over the careful delineation of leaf and cloud after the manner of the Japanese. The details are not visible, but felt. He rarely lays stress on minor points; but if he does so, it is with the same sense of congruity that a great composer reiterates a motive in music. Turguenief's enemies make ground of this very dexterity, which is displayed in all his works, for denying him originality, — as though originality must need be independent of the eternal laws of proportion and harmony which are the natural measures of beauty.

Ernest Renan pronounced quite another opinion, however, when, according to the custom of the French, he delivered a discourse over the tomb that was about to receive the mortal remains of Turguenief, on the 1st of October, 1883. He said that Turguenief was not the conscience of one individual, but in a certain sense that of a whole people, — the incarnation of a race, the voice of past generations that slept the sleep of ages until he evoked them. For the multitude is silent, and the poet or the prophet must serve as its interpreter; and Turguenief holds this attitude to the great Sclavonic race, whose entrance upon the world's stage is the most astounding event of our century. Divided by its own magnitude, the Sclav race is united in the great soul and the conciliatory spirit of Turguenief, Genius having accomplished in a day that which Time could not do in ages. He has created an atmosphere of beautiful peace, wherein those who fought as mortal enemies may meet and clasp each other by the hand.

It was just this impartiality and universality, which Renan praises so highly, that alienated from Turguenief many of his contemporaries and compatriots. Where ideas are at war, whoever takes a neutral position makes himself the enemy to both parties. Turguenief knew this, and he used sometimes to say, on hearing the bitter judgments passed upon him, "Let them do what they like: my soul is not in their hands." Not only the revolutionaries took it ill that he did not explicitly cast his adhesion with them, but the country at large, whose national pride spurned foreign civilization, was offended at the candor and realism of his observations. And Turguenief, though Russian every inch of him, loved Latin culture, and had developed and perfected by association with French writers, such as Prosper Merimée and Gustave Flaubert, those qualities of precision, clearness, and skill in composition, which distinguish him above all his countrymen; yet this was a serious offence to the most of these latter.

Among modern French novelists, those who, to my mind, most resemble Turguenief in the nature of their talents, are, first, Daudet, for intensity of emotion and richness of design, and then the brothers Goncourt in some, though not very many, pages. Yet there is a notable difference in all. Daudet is less the epic poet than Turguenief, because he devotes himself to the study of certain special aspects of Parisian life, while Turguenief takes in the whole physiognomy of his immense country. From the laboring peasants and the nihilist students to the generals and government clerks, he depicts every condition, — except the highest society, which has been reserved for Leon Tolstoï. And everything is vivid, interesting, fascinating, — the poor paralytic of "Living Relics," as well as the courageous heroine of "Virgin Soil," — everything is real as well as poetical. Truth and poetry are united in him as closely as soul and body. Though he is an indefatigable observer, he never tires the reader; his heart overflowed with sentiment, yet his good taste never permitted him to utter a false note either of brutality or cant; he was a most eloquent advocate of emancipation, moderation, and peace, yet no diatribe of either a social or political character ever ruffled the celestial calm of his muse. Puchkine and Turguenief are, to my mind, the two Russian spirits worthy to be called *classic.*

Those who knew him and associated with him speak of his goodness as one speaks of a mountain's height when gazing upward from its foot. Voguié calls him a heavenly soul, one of the poor in spirit burning with the fire of inspiration, one who seemed, amid the hard and selfish world, the vain and jealous world of French letters, a visionary with gaze distraught and heart unsullied, a member of some shepherd tribe or patriarchal family. Every Russian that arrived penniless in Paris went straight to his house for protection and assistance.

II.

GONTCHAROF AND OBLOMOVISM.

THE rival and competitor of Turguenief — not in Europe, but in Russia — was a novelist of whom I must say something at least, though I do not consider that he holds a place among the great masters; I mean Gontcharof. This author's talents were fostered under the influence of the famous critic Bielinsky, who professed and taught the principles promulgated by Gogol, — demanded that art should be a faithful representation of life, and its principal object the study of the people.

Ivan Gontcharof was not of the nobility, like Turguenief, but came of a family of traders, and was born in the critical year of 1812. His life was humble and laborious; he was a tutor, and then a government employee, and made a tour of the world aboard the frigate "Pallas." He began his literary career in the middle of that most glorious decade for Russian letters known as "the forties." His first novel, entitled "A Vulgar History," attracted public attention, and it is said that a secret notice from the imperial censor in consequence was the cause of the long silence of twelve years which the author maintained until the time when he wrote "Oblomof," which is, to my mind, one of the most pleasing and characteristic Russian novels. I must admit that I am acquainted with only the first volume of it, for the simple reason that it is the only one translated; and I must add that this volume begins with the moment when the hero awakes from sleep, and ends with his resolve to get up and dress and go out into the street! Yet this odd little volume has an indescribable charm, an intensity of feeling which takes the place of action, and incidents as easily invented by the idealist as observed by the realist. In these days the art of story-telling has undergone a great change; the hero no longer keeps a dagger, a cup of poison, rope-ladders, and rivals at hand, but he runs to the other extreme, not less trivial and puerile perhaps, of exaggerating small incidents that are uninteresting, and irrelevant to the subject or the essential thought of the work from an artistic point of view. But in "Oblomof," whose hero does nothing but lie still in bed, there is not a detail or a line that is superfluous to the harmonious effect of the whole. Of course I can only speak of the one volume I have read. One may imagine that the author would like to portray the state of enervation and disorganization to which the essence of autocratic despotism had brought Russian society; or perhaps it is one aspect of the Russian soul, the dreamy indolence and insuperable apathy of the body, which weighs down the active work of the imagination. It is only a study of a psychical condition, yet what intense life throbs in its pages!

Perhaps this admirable and original novel was not translated in its entirety for fear of offending French taste, which demands more excitement, and could not stand a long analytical narrative full of detail, mere intellectual filigree. Turguenief was undeniably a greater artist than his rival; but he never attained to the precision, lucidity, and singular strength of "Oblomof" in any of his novels.

As the character of the hero was drawn to the life, the nation recognized it at once, and the word *oblomovism* became incorporated into the language, implying the typical indolence of the Sclav. On some accounts I find Turguenief's "Living Relics" more comparable to this novel than any others of his. Both present one single phase or state of the soul; both are purely psychological studies; the chief character of both does not change position, the position in which he has been fixed by the will of the novelist, —I had almost said the dissecting surgeon.

"Oblomof" is in reality a type of the Sclav who chases the butterfly of his dreams through the still air. Study he regards, from his pessimist point of view, as useless, because it will not lead him to earthly happiness; and yet his soul is full of poetry and his heart of tenderness; he reaches out toward illimitable horizons, and his imagination is hard at work, but all his other faculties are asleep.

III.

DOSTOIËWSKY, PSYCHOLOGIST AND VISIONARY.

Now let us turn to that visionary novelist whom Voguié introduces to his readers in these words :

"Here comes the Scythian, the true Scythian, who puts off the habiliments of our modern intellect, and leads us by the hand to the centre of Moscow, to the monstrous Cathedral of St. Basil, wrought and painted like a Chinese pagoda, built by Tartar architects, and yet consecrated to the God whom the Christians adore. Dostoiëwsky was educated at the same school, led by the same current of thought, and made his first appearance in the same year as Turguenief and Tolstoï; but the latter are opposite poles, and have but one ground in common, which is the sympathy for humanity, which was incarnate and expanded in Dostoiëwsky to the highest degree of piety, to pious despair, if such a phrase is possible."

Dostoiëwsky is really the barbarian, the primitive type, whose heart-strings still reverberate certain motive tones of the Russian soul that were incompatible with the harmonious and tranquil spirit of Turguenief. Dostoiëwsky has the feverish, unreasoning, abnormal psychological intensity of the cultivated minds of his country. Let no one of tender heart and weak nerves read his books; and those who cling to classic serenity, harmony, and brightness should not so much as touch them. He leads us into a new region of æsthetics, where the horrible is beautiful, despair is consoling, and the ignoble has a halo of sublimity: where guilty women teach gospel truths, and men are regenerated by crimes; where the prison is the school of compassion, and fetters are a poetic element. Much against our will we are forced to admire a novelist whose pages almost excite to assassination and nightmare horrors, this Russian Dante who will not allow us to omit a single circle of the Inferno.

Feodor, son of Michael Dostoiëwsky, was born in Moscow in 1821, in a hospital at which his father was a medical attendant. There is frequently a strange connection between the environment of great writers and the development and direction of their genius, not always evident to the general public, but apparent to the careful critic; in Dostoiëwsky's case it seems plain enough to all, however. His family belonged to the country gentlefolk from whom the class of government employees are drawn; Feodor, with his brother Alexis, whom he dearly loved, entered the school of military engineers, though his tastes were rather for belles-lettres and the humanities than for dry and unartistic details. His literary education was therefore reduced to fitful readings of Balzac, Eugene Sue, George Sand, and especially of Gogol, whose works first inspired him with tenderness toward the humble, the outcast, and the miserable. Shortly after leaving college he abandoned his career for a literary life, and began the usual struggle with the difficulties of a young writer's precarious condition. The struggle lasted almost to the end of his life; for forty years he was never sure of any other than prison bread. Proud and suspicious by nature, the humiliations and bitterness of poverty must have contributed largely to unsettle his nerves, disconcert his mind, and undermine his health, which was so precarious that he used sometimes to leave on his table before going to sleep a paper with the words: "I may fall into a state of insensibility to-night; do not bury me until some days have passed." He was sometimes afflicted with epilepsy, cruelly aggravated later in Siberia under the lashes laid upon his bleeding shoulders.

Like one of his own heroes he dreamed of fame; and without having read or shown his manuscripts to any one, alone with his chimeras and vagaries, he passed whole nights in imaginary intercourse with the characters he created, loving them as though they had been his relatives or his friends, and weeping over their misfortunes as though they had been real. These were hours of pure emotion, ideal love, which every true artist experiences some time in his life. Dostoïewsky was then twenty-three years old. One day he begged a friend to take a few chapters of his first novel called "The Poor People" to the popular poet Nekrasof; his friend did so, and in the early hours of the morning the famous poet called at the door of the unknown writer and clasped him in his arms under the excitement of the emotion caused by perusal of the story. Nekrasof did not remit his attentions; he at once sought the dreaded critic Bielinsky, the intellectual chief and lawgiver of the glorious company of writers to which Turguenief, Tolstoï, and Gontcharof belonged, the Russian Lessing, who died of consumption at the age of thirty-eight years, just when others are beginning to acquire discernment and tranquillity, — the great Bielinsky, who had formed two generations of great artists and pushed forward the national literature to a complete development. A man in his position, more prone to meet with the sham than the genuine in art, would naturally be not over-delighted to receive people armed with rolls of manuscript. When Nekrasof entered his room exclaiming, "A new Gogol is born to us!" the critic replied in a bad humor, "Gogols are born nowadays as easily as mushrooms in a cellar." But when the author came in a tremor to learn the dictum of the judge, the latter cried out impetuously, "Young man, do you understand how much truth there is in what you have written? No, for you are scarcely more than twenty years old, and it is impossible that you should understand. It is a revelation of art, a gift of Heaven. Respect this gift, and you will be a great writer!" The success achieved by this novel on its publication in the columns of a review did not belie Bielinsky's prophecy.

It is easy to understand the surprise of the critic on reading this work of a scarcely grown man, who yet seemed to have observed life with a vivid and deep sense of realism, and an unequivocal minuteness that is generally learned only through the bitter experience of prosaic sufferings, and comes forth after the illusions and vague sentimentalities of youth have been dispelled and practical life has begun. I said once, and I repeat it, that a true artist under twenty-five would be a marvel; Dostoiëwsky was indeed such a marvel.

This first novel was the humble drama of two lonely souls, wounded and ground down by poverty, but not spoiled by it; a case such as one might meet with on turning the very next corner, and never think worthy of attention or study, and which, even in the midst of modern currents of thought, the novelist is quite likely to pass by. Yet the book is a work of art, — of the new and the old art compounded, classic art infused with the new warm blood of truth. This work of Dostoiëwsky, this touching, tearful story, had a model in Gogol's "The Cloak," but it goes beyond the latter in energy and depth of sadness. If Dostoiëwsky ever invoked a muse, it must have been the muse of Hypochondria.

It was not likely that Dostoiëwsky would escape the political fatality which pursued the generality of Russian writers. During those memorable *forties* the students were wont to meet more or less secretly for the purpose of reading and discussing Fourier, Louis Blanc, and Proudhon. About 1847 these circles began to expand, and to admit public and military men; they were moved by one desire, and what began as an intellectual effervescence ended in a conspiracy. Dostoiëwsky was good material for any

revolutionary cabal, being easily disposed thereto by
his natural enmity to society, his continuous poverty,
his nervous excitement, his Utopian dreams, and his
inordinate and fanatical compassion for the outcast
classes. The occasion was ill-timed, and the hour a
dangerous one, being just at the time of the French
outbreak, which seemed a menace to every throne in
Europe. The police got wind of it, and on the 23d
of April, 1849, thirty-four suspected persons were
arrested, the brothers Feodor and Alexis Dostoiëwsky
among them. The novelist was thrown into a dungeon of the citadel, and when at last he came forth,
it was to mount the scaffold in a public square with
some of his companions. They stood there in shirt-sleeves, in an intense cold, expecting at first only to
hear read the sentence of the Council of War. While
they waited, Dostoiëwsky began to relate to a friend
the plan of a new novel he had been thinking about
in prison; but he suddenly exclaimed, as he heard
the officer's voice, "Is it possible we are to be executed?" His friend pointed to a car-load of objects
which, though covered with a cloth, were shaped
much like coffins. The suspicion was soon confirmed; the prisoners were all tied to posts, and the
soldiers formed in line ready to fire. Suddenly, as
the order was about to be given, word arrived from
the emperor commuting the death-sentence to exile
to Siberia. The prisoners were untied. One of
them had lost his reason.

Dostoiëwsky and the others then set out upon their
sad journey; on arriving at Tobolsk they were each

shaved, laden with chains, and sent to a different station. During this painful experience a pathetic incident occurred which engraved itself indelibly upon the mind of the novelist, and is said to have largely influenced his works. The wives of the "Decembrists" (conspirators of twenty-five years before), most of them women of high rank who had voluntarily exiled themselves in order to accompany their husbands, came to visit in prison the new generation of exiles, and having nothing of material value to offer them, they gave each one a copy of the Gospels. During his four years of imprisonment, Dostoiëwsky never slept without this book under his pillow; he read it incessantly, and taught his more ignorant fellow-prisoners to read it also.

He now found himself among outcasts and convicts, and his ears were filled with the sounds of unknown languages and dialects, and speech which, when understood, was profane and abhorrent, and mixed with yells and curses more dreadful than all complaints. What horrible martyrdom for a man of talent and literary vocation, — reckoned with evildoers, compelled to grind gypsum, and deprived of every means of satisfying the hunger and activity of his mind! Why did he not go mad? Some may answer, because he was that already, — and perhaps they would not be far wrong; for no writer in Russia, not excepting even Gogol and Tolstoï, so closely approaches the mysterious dividing line, thin as a hair, which separates insanity and genius. The least that can be said is, that if Dostoiëwsky was not subject to mental aberration from childhood, he had a violent form of neurosis. He was a bundle of nerves, a harp with strings too tense; he was a victim of epilepsy and hallucinations, and the results are apparent in his life and in his books. But it is a strange fact that he himself said that had it not been for the terrible trials he endured, for the sufferings of the prison and the scaffold, he certainly *would have gone mad*, and he believed that these experiences fortified his mind; for, the year previous to his captivity, he declared that he suffered a terrible temptation of the Devil, was a victim to chimerical infirmities, and overwhelmed with an inexplicable terror which he calls *mystic fear*, and thus describes in one of his novels: "On the approach of twilight I was attacked by a state of soul which frequently comes upon me in the night; I will call it *mystic fear*. It is an overwhelming terror of *something* which I can neither define nor imagine, which has no existence in the natural order of things, but which I feel may at any moment become real, and appear before me as an inexorable and horrible *thing*." It seems then quite possible that the writer was cured of his imaginary ills by real ones.

I have remarked that Gogol's "Dead Souls" reminded me of "Don Quixote" more than any book I know; let me add that the book inspired by the prison-life of Dostoiëwsky — "The Dead House" — reminds me most strongly of Dante's Inferno. There is no exact likeness or affinity of literary style; for "The Dead House" is not a poem, but a plain tale of the sufferings of a few prisoners in a miserable Siberian fort. And yet it is certainly *Dantesque*. Instead of the laurel-crowned poet in scholar's gown, led by the bright genius of antiquity, we see the wistful-eyed, tearful Sclav, his compressed lips, his attitude of resignation, and in his hands a copy of the Gospels; but the Florentine and the Russian manifest the same melancholy energy, use the same burin to trace their burning words on plates of bronze, and unite a prophetic vision with a brutal realism of miserable and sinful humanity.

"The Dead House" also has the merit of being perhaps the most profound study written in Europe upon the penitentiary system and criminal physiology; it is a more powerful teacher of jurists and legislators than all didactic treatises. Dostoiëwsky shows especially, and with implacable clearness, the effect produced on the minds of the prisoners by the cruel penalty of the lash. The complacency of narration, the elaborateness of detail, the microscopic precision with which he notes every phase of this torture, inflict positive pain upon the nervous system of the reader. It is fascinating, it is the refinement of barbarism, but it was also a work of charity, for it finally brought about the abolition of that kind of punishment, and wiped out a foul stain upon the Russian Code. It makes one turn cold and shudder to read those pages which describe this torture, — so calmly and carefully related without one exclamation of pity or comment, and even sometimes painfully humorous. The trepidation of the condemned for days before it is inflicted, his frenzy after it is over, his subterfuges to avoid it, the blind fury with which sometimes he yields to it, throwing himself under the painful blows as a despairing man throws himself into the sea, — these are word-pictures never to be forgotten.

Voguié makes a striking comparison of the different fates awarded to certain books, and says that while "My Prisons," by Silvio Pellico, went all over the world, this autobiographical fragment by Dostoiëwsky was unknown to Europe until very recently; yet it is far superior in sincerity and energy to that of the Italian prisoner. The most interesting and moving stories of captivity that I know of are Russian, and chief among them I would mention "Memories of a Nihilist," by Paulowsky. The tone of resignation, of melancholy simplicity, in all these tales, however, is sure to touch all hearts. I will not quote a line from "The Dead House;" it must be read, attentively and patiently, and, like most Russian books, it has not the merit of brevity. But the style is so shorn of artifice and rhetorical pretension, and the story runs along so unaffectedly, that I cannot select any one page as an example of excellence; for the excellence of the book depends on the whole, — on the accumulated force of observation, on the complete aspect of a soul that feels deeply and sees clearly, — and we must not break the icy ring of Siberian winter which encloses it. It is enhanced by the apparent serenity of the writer, by his sweetness, his half-Christian, half-Buddhist resignation. With the Gospels in his hand, Dostoiëwsky at last leaves his house of pain, without rancor or hatred or choleric protests; more than this, he leaves it declaring that the trial has been beneficial to him, that it has regenerated body and soul; that in prison he has learned to love the brethren, and to find the spark of goodness and truth lighted by God's hand even in the souls of reprobates and criminals; to know the charity that passes understanding and the pity that is foolishness to the wise; he has learned, in fact, *to love*, — the only learning that can redeem the condemned.

Although he had been (at the time of writing this) four years released from prison, he delayed still six years longer before returning to Europe to publish his works. When he began his labors for the press, he did not unite himself to the liberal party, but, erratic as usual, he turned to the Sclavophiles, — the blind lovers of old usages and customs, the bitter enemies of the civilization of the Occident. Fate was not yet weary in persecuting him. After the death of his wife and brother he was obliged to flee the country on account of his creditors. His sorrows were not exactly of the sublime nature of Puchkine's and the melancholy poet's; they were on the contrary very prosaic, — lack of money, combined with terrible fits of epilepsy. To understand the mortifications of poverty to a proud and sensitive man, one must read Dostoiëwsky's correspondence, — so like Balzac's in its incessant complaints against pecuniary affairs. He exclaims, "The details of my poverty are shameful. I cannot relate them. Sometimes I spend the whole night walking my room like a caged beast, tearing my hair in despair. I must have such or such a sum to-morrow, without fail!" Gloomy and ill, he wandered through Germany, France, and Italy, caring nothing for the wonders of civilization, and impressed by no sights except the guillotine. He wrote during this time his three principal novels, whose very names are nightmares, — " Possessed with Devils," "The Idiot," and " Crime and Punishment."

I know by experience the diabolical power of Dostoiëwsky's psychological analysis. His books make one ill, although one appear to be well. No wonder that they exercise a perturbing influence on Russian imaginations, which are only too prone to hallucination and mental ecstasy. I will briefly mention his best and most widely known book, " Crime and Punishment," of which the following is the argument: A student commits a crime, and then voluntarily confesses it to the magistrate. This seems neither more nor less than an ordinary notice in the newspaper, but what an analysis is conveyed by means of it! It is horrible to think that the sentiments so studiously wrought out can be human, and that we all carry the germs of them hidden in some corner of the soul; and not only human, but possessed even by a person of great intellectual culture, like the hero, whose crime is the result of great reading reduced to horrible sophisms. Those two Parisian students who, after saturating their minds with Darwin and Haeckel, cut a woman to pieces with their bistouries, must have been prototypes of Rodion Romanovitch, the hero of this novel of Dostoiëwsky. This young man is not only clever, but possesses really refined sentiments; one of the motives that lead to his crime is that one of his sisters, the most dearly loved, may have to marry an unworthy man in order to insure the welfare of the family. Such a *sale* as this poor girl's marriage would be seems to the student a greater wrong than the assassination of the old money-lender. The first seed of the crime falls upon his soul on overhearing at a wine-shop a dialogue between another student and an officer. "Here you have on the one hand," says the student, "an old woman, sick, stupid, wicked, useful to nobody, and only doing harm to all the world about her, who does not know what she lives for, and who, when you least expect it, will die a natural death; you have on the other hand a young creature whose strength is being wasted for lack of sustenance, a hundred lives that might be guided into a right path, dozens of families that might be saved from destitution, dissolution, ruin, and vice if that old woman's money were only available. If somebody were to kill her and use her fortune for the good of humanity, do you not think that a thousand good deeds would compensate for the crime? It is a mathematical question. What weight has a stupid, evil-minded old shrew in the social scale? About as much as a bed-bug."

"Without doubt," replies the officer, "the old woman does not deserve to live. But — what can you do? Nature — "

"My friend," the other replies, "Nature can be

corrected and amended. If it were not so we should all be buried to the neck in prejudices, and there would not be a great man amongst us."

This atrocious ratiocination takes hold upon Rodion's mind, and he carries it out to terribly logical consequences. Napoleon sacrificed thousands of men on the altar of his genius; why had he not the right to sacrifice one ridiculous old woman to his own great needs? The ordinary man must not infringe the law; but the extraordinary man may authorize his conscience to do away with certain obstacles in his path.

It has been said that Dostoiëwsky's talents were influenced in some measure by the fascinating personality of Edgar Poe. The analogies are apparent; but the author of "The Gold Beetle," with all his suggestive intensity and his feverish imagination, never achieved any such tremendous psychological analyses as those of "Crime and Punishment." It is impossible to select an example from it; every page is full of it. The temptation that precedes the assassination, the horrible moment of committing it, the manner of disposing of the traces of it, the agonizing terror of being discovered, the instinct which leads him back to the scene of the crime with no motive but to yield to a desire as irresistible as inexplicable, his fearful visit to the place where he lives over again the moment when he plunged the knife into the old woman's skull, — examining all the furniture, laying his hand upon the bell again, with a fiendish enjoyment of the sound of it, and looking again for the marks of blood on the floor, — it is too well done; it makes one excited, nervous, and ill.

"Is this beautiful?" some will ask. All that Dostoiëwsky has written bears the same character; it wrings the soul, perverts the imagination, overturns one's ideas of right and wrong to an incredible degree. Sometimes one is lost in abysms of gloomy uncertainty, like Hamlet; again one sees the struggle of the evil genius against Providence, like Faust, or a soul lacerated by remorse like Macbeth; and all his heroes are fools, madmen, maniacs, and philosophers of hypochondria and desperation. And yet I say that this is beauty, — tortured, twisted, Satanic, but intense, grand, and powerful. Dostoiëwsky's are bad books to read during digestion, or on going to bed at night, when every dim object takes an unusual shape, and every breath stirs the window curtains; they are not good books to take to the country, where one sits under the spreading trees with a fresh and fragrant breeze and a soul expanded with contentment, and one thanks God only to be alive. But they are splendid books for the thinker who devours them with reflective attention, — his brow furrowed under the light of the student-lamp, and feeling all around him the stir and excitement of a great city like Paris or St. Petersburg.

But there is a drop of balm in the cup of absinthe to which we may liken Dostoiëwsky's books; it is the Christianity which appears in them when and where its consoling presence is least expected. Face to face with the student who becomes a criminal through pride and injudicious reading, we see the figure of a pure, modest, pious girl, who redeems him by her love. This unfortunate girl is a flower that fades before its time; it is she who, being sacrificed to provide bread for her family, comes in time to convince the criminal of his sin, enlightens his mind with the lamp of the Gospels, and brings him to repentance, resignation, and the joy of regeneration, in the expiation of his crime by chastisement and the dungeon.

There is one marked difference between "Crime and Punishment" and "The Dead House." The novel is feverish, the autobiography is calm. Dostoiëwsky is a madman who owes his lucid intervals to tribulations and torture. Suffering clears his mind and alleviates his pain; tears sweeten his bitterness, and sorrow is his supreme religion; like his student hero, he prostrates himself before human suffering.

The best way of taking the measure of Dostoiëwsky's personality is to compare him with his competitor and rival, and perhaps his enemy, Ivan Turguenief. There could be no greater contrast. Turguenief is above all an artist, almost classic in his serenity, master of the arts of form, delicate, refined, exquisite, a perfect scene-painter, an always interesting narrator, reasonable and temperately liberal in his opinions, optimist, or, if I may be allowed the word, Olympic, to the extent that he could boast of being able to die tranquilly because he had enjoyed all that was truly beautiful in life. Dostoiëwsky is a rabid psychologist, almost an enemy to Nature and the sensuous world, a furious and implacable painter of prisons, hospitals, public houses and by-streets of great cities, awkward in his style, taking only a one-sided view of character, a revolutionary and yet a reactionary in politics, and not only adverse to every sort of paganism, but hazily mystical, — the apostle of redemption through suffering, and of the compassion which seeks wounds to cure with its healing lips. Their two lives are correlative to their characters, — Turguenief in the Occident, famous and fortunate; Dostoiëwsky in the Orient, a barbarian, the plaything of destiny, fighting with poverty shoulder to shoulder. It was only natural that sooner or later the two novelists should know each other as enemies. It is sad to relate that Dostoiëwsky attacked Turguenief in so furious a manner that it can only be attributed to envy and malice.

In his own country, however, and in respect to his popularity and influence with young people, the author of "Crime and Punishment" ranked higher than the author of "Virgin Soil." Just in proportion as Turguenief was attractive to us in the West, Dostoiëwsky fascinated the people of his country. "Crime and Punishment" was an event in Russia. Dostoiëwsky had the honor — if honor it may be called — of dealing a blow upon the soul of his compatriots, and on this account, as he himself used sometimes to say, especially after his epileptic attacks, he felt himself to be a great criminal, and the guilt of a villanous act weighed upon his soul; and it happened that a certain student, after reading his book, thought himself possessed by the same impulses as the hero, and committed a murder with the same circumstances and details.

After writing "Crime and Punishment, Dostoiëwsky's talent declined; his defects became more marked, his psychology more and more involved and painful, his heroes more insensate, lunatic, epileptic, and overwrought, absorbed in inexplicable contemplations, or wandering, rapt in delirious dreams, through the streets. His novels are, in fact, the antechamber to the madhouse. But we may once more notice the influence of Cervantes on Russian minds; for the most important character created by Dostoiëwsky, after the hero of "Crime and Punishment," is a type, imitated after Quixote, in "The Idiot," — a righter of wrongs, a fool, or rather a sublime innocent.

As much as Dostoiëwsky excels in originality, he lacks in rhythm and harmony. His way of looking at the world is the way of the fever-stricken. No one has carried realism so far; but his may be called a mystic realism. Neither he nor his heroes belong to our light-loving race or our temperate civilization; they are the outcome of Russian exuberance, to us almost incomprehensible. He is at one moment an apostle, at another a maniac, now a philosopher, then a fanatic. Voguié, in describing his physiognomy, says: "Never have I seen in any other face such an expression of accumulated suffering; all the agonies of flesh and spirit were stamped upon it; one read in it, better than in any book, the recollection of the prison, the long habits of terror, torture, and anguish.

When he was angry, one seemed to see him in the prisoner's dock. At other times his countenance had the sad meekness of the aged saints in Russian sacred pictures."

In his last years Dostoiëwsky was the idol of the youth of Russia, who not only awaited his novels most eagerly, but ran to consult him as they would a spiritual director, entreating his advice or consolation. The prestige of Turguenief was for the moment eclipsed. Tolstoï found his audience chiefly among *the intelligence*, and Dostoiëwsky of the lacerated heart was the object of the love and devotion of the new generation. When the monument to Puchkine was unveiled, in 1880, the popularity of Dostoiëwsky was at its height; when he spoke, the people sobbed in sympathy; they carried him in triumph; the students assaulted the drawing-rooms that they might see him near by, and one even fainted with ecstasy on touching him.

He died, February 10, 1881, almost crazed with patriotic love and enthusiasm, like Gogol. The multitudes fought for the flowers that were strewn over his grave, as precious relics. His obsequies were an imposing manifestation. In a land without liberty this novelist was the Messiah of the new generations.

IV.

TOLSTOÏ, NIHILIST AND MYSTIC.

THE youngest of the four great Russian novelists, the only one living to-day, and in general opinion the most excellent, is Leon, son of Nicholas Count Tolstoï. His biography may be put into a few lines; it has no element of the dramatic or curious. He was born in 1828; he was brought up, like most Russian noblemen of his class, in the country, on his patrimonial estates; he pursued his studies at the University of Kazan, receiving the cosmopolitan education — half French, half German — which is the nursery of the Russian aristocracy; he entered the military career, spent some years in the Caucasus attached to a regiment of artillery, was transferred to Sevastopol at his own desire, and witnessed there the memorable siege, the heroes of which he has immortalized in three of his volumes; on the conclusion of the peace he dedicated some time to travel; he resided by turns at both Russian capitals, frequenting the best society, his congenial atmosphere, yet without being captivated by it; he finally renounced the life of the world, married in 1860, and retired to his possessions near Toula, where he has lived in his own way for twenty-five years or more, and where to-day the famous novelist, the gentleman, the scholar, the sceptic, — after falling like Saul on the road to Damascus, blinded by a heavenly vision, and being converted, as he himself says,— shows himself, to all who go to visit him, dressed in peasant's garb, swinging the scythe or drawing the sickle.

The more important biography of Count Tolstoï is that which pertains to his soul, always restless, always in pursuit of absolute truth and the divine essence,— a noble aspiration which ameliorates even error. There is no book of Tolstoï's but reveals himself, particularly so the autobiography entitled "My Memories," and certain passages of his novels, and lastly, his theologico-moral works. Tolstoï belongs to the class of souls that without God lose their hold on life; and yet, by his own confession, the novelist lived without any sort of faith or creed from his youth to maturity.

Ever since the time when Tolstoï saw the dreams of his childhood vanish, — began to think for himself, and to experience the religious crisis which usually arrives between the ages of fifteen and twenty-five, — his soul, like a storm-tossed bark, has oscillated between pantheism and the blackest pessimism. What depths of despair a soul like that of Tolstoï can know, unable to rest upon the pillow of doubt, when it abnegates the noblest of human faculties,— thought and intelligence, — and makes choice of a merely vegetative life in preference to that of the rational being! Lost in the gloom of this dark wilderness, he falls into the region of absolute nihilism. He admits this in his confessions ("My Religion") when he says : " For thirty-five years of my life I have been a nihilist in the rigorous acceptation of the term ; that is to say, not merely a revolutionary socialist, but a man who believes in nothing whatever."

In fact, since the age of sixteen, as we read in his "Memoirs," his mind summoned to judgment all accepted and consecrated doctrines and philosophical opinions, and that which most suited the boy was scepticism, or rather a sort of transcendental egoism; he allows himself to think that nothing exists in the world but himself; that exterior objects are vain apparitions, no longer real to his mind; impressed and persuaded by this fixed idea, he believes he sees, materially, behind and all around him, the abyss of nothingness, and under the effect of this hallucination he falls into a state of mind that might be called truly motor madness, though it was transitory and momentary, — a state proper to the visionary peoples of the North, and to which they give an involved appellation difficult to pronounce; to translate it exactly, with all its shades of signification, I should have to mix and mingle together many words of ours, such as despair, fatalism, asceticism, intractability, brief delirium, lunacy, mania, hypochondria, and frenzy, — a species of dementia, in fine, which, snapping the mainspring of human will, induces inexplicable acts, such as throwing one's self into an abyss, setting fire to a house for the pleasure of it, holding the muzzle of a pistol to one's forehead and thinking, "Shall I pull the trigger?" or, on seeing a person of distinction, to pull him by the nose and shake him like a child. This momentary but real dementia — from which nobody is perhaps entirely exempt, and which Shakespeare has so admirably analyzed in some scenes of "Hamlet" — is to the individual what panic is to the multitude, or like *epidemia chorea*, or a suicidal monomania which sometimes seems to be in the air; its origin lies deep in the mysterious recesses of our moral being, where other strange psychical phenomena are hidden, such as, for example, the fascination of seeing blood flow, and the innate love of destruction and death.

But let us turn to the real literary work of Tolstoï before referring to the actual cause of his perturbed conscience. After the beautiful story called "The Cossacks," he prepared himself, by other short novels, for works of larger importance. Among the former should be mentioned the sweet story of "Katia," which already reveals the profound reader of the human heart and the great realist writer. For Tolstoï, who knows how to cover vast canvases with vivid colors, is no less successful in small pictures; and his short novels, "The Death of Ivan Iliitch" and the first part of "The Horse's Romance," for example, are hardly to be excelled. But his fame was chiefly assured by two great works, — "War and Peace" and "Anna Karénina." The former is a sort of cosmorama of Russian society before and during the French invasion, a series of pictures that might be called Russian national episodes. Like our own Galdos, Tolstoï studied the formative epoch of modern society, the heroic age in which the Great Captain of the century awoke in the nations of Europe, while endeavoring to subjugate them, a national conscience, just as he transmitted to them, though unwittingly, the impetus of the French Revolution. Russia heroically resisting the outsider is Tolstoï's hero.

The action of the novel merely serves as a pretext to intertwine chapters of history, politics, and philosophy; it is rather a general panorama of Russian life than an artistic fiction. "War and Peace" is a complement to the poetic satire of Gogol, delineating the new society which was to rise upon the ruins of the past. If we apply the rules of composition in novel-writing, "War and Peace" cannot be defended; there is neither unity, nor hero, nor hardly plot; so loose and careless is the thread that binds the story together, and so slowly does the argument develop, that sometimes the reader has already forgotten the name of a character when he meets with it again ten chapters farther on. The vast incoherence of the Russian soul, its lack of mental discipline, its vagueness and liking for digressions, could have no more complete personification in literature.

One therefore needs resolution to plunge into the perusal of works in which art mimics Nature, copying the illimitable extension of the Russian plains. I once asked a very clever friend how she was occupying herself. She replied, "I have fallen to the bottom of a Russian novel, and I cannot get out!" But scarcely has one finished the first two hundred pages, as a first mouthful, when one's interest begins to awaken,—not a mere vulgar curiosity as to events, but a noble interest of mind and heart. It is the stream of life, grand and majestic, which passes before our eyes like the expanse of a mighty flowing river.

Tolstoï — more than Turguenief, who is always and first of all the artist, and more than Dostoiëwsky, who sees humanity from the point of view of his own turbulent mind and confused soul — Tolstoï produces a supreme and absolute impression of the truth, although, in the light of his harmonious union of faculties, it is impossible to say whether he hits the mark by means of external or internal realism, — whether he is more perfect in his descriptions, his dialogues, or his studies of character. In reading Tolstoï, we feel as though we were looking at the spectacle of the universe where nothing seems to us unreal or invented.

Tolstoï's fictitious characters are not more vivid than his historical ones, — Napoleon or Alexander I., for example; he is as careful in the expression of a sublime sentiment as in a minute and vulgar detail. Every touch is wonderful. His description of a battle is amazing (and who else can describe a battle like Tolstoï!), but he is charming when he gives us the day-dreams and love-fancies of a child still playing with her dolls. And what a clear intuition he has of the motives of human actions! What a penetrating, unwavering, scrutinizing glance that "trieth the hearts and the reins," as saith the Scripture! Tolstoï does not exhaust his perspicacity in the study of instinct alone; with eagle eye he pierces the most complex souls, refined and enveloped in the veil of education, — courtiers, diplomats, princes, generals, ladies of high rank, and famous statesmen. No one else has described the drawing-room so exquisitely and so truly as Tolstoï; and it must be admitted that the picture of official good society is terribly embarrassing. Some chapters of "Anna Karénina" and "War and Peace" seem to exhale the warm soft air that greets us as we enter the door of a luxurious, aristocratic mansion. The master-painter controls the collectivity as well as the individual; he dissects the soul of the multitude, the spirit of the nation, with the same energy and dexterity as that of one man. The wonderful pictures of the invasion and burning of Moscow are continual examples of this.

Is "War and Peace" a historical novel in the limited, archæological, false, and conventional conception? Certainly not. Tolstoï's historical novel has realized the conjunction of the novel and the epic, with the good qualities of both. In this novel — so broad, so deep, so human, and at times so patriotic, as Tolstoï understands patriotism — there is a subtle breath of nihilism, an essence of euphorbia, a poison of *ourare*, which colors the whole drift of Russian literature. This tendency is personified in the hero (if the book may be said to have one at all), Pierre Besukof, a true Sclavonic soul, expansive, full of unrest and disquietude, passionate, unstable, the character of a child united to the investigating intelligence of a philosopher, — a pre-nihilist (to coin a word) who goes in search of certainty and repose, and finds them not until he meets at last with one "poor in spirit," a wretched common soldier, a type of meek resignation and inconsequent fatalism, who shows him how to attain to his desires through a mystic indifferentism, a voluntary abrogation of the body, and a vegetative form of existence, in fact, a form of quietism, of Indian Nirvana.

This same philosophical concept inspires all of Tolstoï's writings. Once a nihilist and now converted, culture and the exercise of reason are to him lamentable gifts; his ideal is not progression, but retrogression; the final word of human wisdom is to return to pure Nature, the eternal type of goodness, beauty, and truth. The Catholic Church has also honored the saintly lives of the poor in spirit, such as Pascual Bailon and Fray Junipero, *the Idiot;* but assuredly it has never presented them as models worthy of imitation in general, only as living examples of grace; and on the contrary, it is the intelligence of great thinkers, like Augustine, Thomas, and Buenaventura, that is revered and written about. In the whole catalogue of sins there is perhaps none more blasphemous than that of spurning the light given by the Creator to every creature. But to return to Tolstoï.

His literary testament is to be found in "Anna Karénina," a novel but little less prolix than "War and Peace," published in 1877. While "War and Peace" pictured society at the beginning of the century, "Anna Karénina" pictures contemporary society, — a more difficult task, because it lacks perspective, yet an easier one, because one can better understand the mode of thought of one's contemporaries; therefore in "Anna Karénina" the epic quality is inferior to the lyric. The principal character is amply developed, and the study of passion is complete and profound.

The argument in "Anna Karénina" is upon an illicit love, young, sincere, and overpowering. Tolstoï does not justify it; the whole tone of the book is austere. It would seem as though he proposed to demonstrate — indirectly, and according to the demands of art — that a generous soul cannot live outside the moral law; and that even when circumstances seem entirely favorable, and those obstacles which society and custom oppose to his passion have disappeared, the discord within him is enough to poison happiness and make life intolerable.

In both of Tolstoï's novels there is much insistence on the necessity of believing and contemplating religious matters, the thirst of faith. Although Tolstoï observes the canon of literary impersonality with a rigorous care that is equal to that of Flaubert himself, yet it is plainly to be seen that Pierre Besukof in "War and Peace," and Levine in "Anna Karénina" are one and the same with the author, with his doubts, his painful anxiety to get away from indifferentism and to solve the eternal problem whose explanation Heine demanded of the waves of the North Sea. Tolstoï cannot consent to the idea of dying an atheist and a nihilist, or to living without knowing why or for what.

Referring to the autobiography called "Memoirs," we see that from childhood he was troubled and tortured by the mystery of things about him and the hereafter. He tells there how his mind reasoned with, penetrated, and passed in review the diverse solutions offered to the great enigma; once he thought, like the Stoics, that happiness depends not upon circumstances, but upon our manner of accepting them, and that a man inured to suffering could not be afflicted by misfortunes; possessed with this idea he held a heavy dictionary upon his outstretched hand for five mintues, enduring frightful pains; he disciplined himself with a whip until his tears started. Then he turned to Epicurus; he remembered that life is short; that to man belongs only the disposition of the present; and under the influence of these ideas he abandoned his lessons for three days, and spent the time lying on his bed reading novels or eating sweets. He sees a horse, and at once inquires, "When this animal dies, where will his spirit go? Into the body of another horse? Into the body of a man?" And he wearies himself with questionings, with struggling over knotty problems, with thoughts upon thoughts, and all the while his ardent imagination conjures before him dreams of love, happiness, and fame.

Beneath the restless effervescence of fancy and youth the religious sentiment was pulsating, — the strongest and most deeply rooted sentiment in his soul. One episode from the "Memoirs" will prove to us the innate religious nature of the novelist. He tells us that once, when he was still a child in his father's country-house, a certain beggar came to the door, a poor vagabond, one-eyed and pock-marked, half idiot and foolish, — one of those coarse clay vessels in which, according to contemporaneous Russian literature, the divine light is wont to be enclosed. He was offered shelter and hospitality, though none knew whence he came, nor why he followed a mysterious wandering life, always going from place to place, barefooted and poor, visiting the convents, distributing religious objects, murmuring incoherent words, and sleeping wherever a handful of straw was thrown down for him. Within the house, at suppertime, they fall to discussing him. Tolstoï's mother pities him, his father abuses him; the latter thinks him little better than a cheat and a sluggard, the former reveres him as one inspired of God, a holy man, who earns glory and reward every minute by wearing around his body a chain sixty pounds in weight. Nevertheless, the vagabond obtains shelter and food, and the children, whose curiosity has been excited by the discussion, go and hide in a dark room next to his, so as "to see Gricha's chain." Tolstoï was filled with awe in his dark corner to hear the beggar pray, to see him throw himself upon the floor and writhe in mystic transports amid the clanking of his chain. "Many things have happened since then," he exclaims, "many other memories have lost all importance for me; Gricha, the wanderer, has long since reached the end of his last journey, but the impression which he produced upon me will never fade; I shall never forget the feelings that he awoke in my soul. O Gricha! O great Christian! Thy faith was so ardent that thou couldst feel God near; thy love was so great that the words flowed of themselves from thy lips, and thou hadst not to ask thy reason for an examination of them. And how magnificently didst thou praise the Almighty when, words failing to express the feelings of thy heart, thou threwest thyself weeping upon the floor!" This episode of childhood will indeed never fade from the memory or the heart of Tolstoï. After seeking conviction and repose in arrogant human science and in philosophy, Tolstoï, like his two heroes, finds them at last in the meekness and simplicity of the most abject classes. Like his own Pierre Besukof, who receives the mystic illumination at the mouth of a common soldier who is to be shot by the French, or like his own Levine, who gets the same from a poor laboring peasant stacking hay, Tolstoï was converted by one Sutayef, one of those innumerable *mujiks* who go about the country announcing the good tidings of the day of communist fraternity. "Five years ago," says Tolstoï in "My Religion," "my faith was given to me; I believed in the teachings of Jesus, and my whole life suddenly changed; I abhorred what I had loved, and loved what I had abhorred; what before seemed bad to me, now seemed good, and *vice versa.*"

It was a sad day for art when this change of spirit came upon Count Tolstoï. Its immediate effect was to suspend the publication of a novel he had begun, to make him despise his master-works, call them empty vanities, and accuse himself of having speculated with the public in arousing evil passions and fanning the fires of sensuality. A heretic and a rationalist (Tolstoï is clearly both; for what he calls

his conversion is neither to Catholicism nor to the
Greek Church), he now abuses the novel, like some
persons nearer home with better intentions than
intelligence, as being an incentive to loose actions,
the Devil's bait, and agrees with Saint Francis de Sales
that "novels are like mushrooms, — the best of them
are good for nothing." Tolstoï has not cast aside the
pen; he continues to write, but no more such superb
pages as we find in "War and Peace" and "Anna
Karénina," no more masterly silhouettes of fine society or the high ranks of the military, not the imperial profile of Alexander I. or the charming figure
of the Princess Marie; he writes edifying apologies,
Biblical parables dedicated to the enlightenment
of village-folk; exegeses and religious controversies,
professions of faith and dramas for the people. Has
the great writer died? Nay, I believe that he still
lives and breathes beneath the coarse tunic and rope
girdle of the peasant-dress he wears, and which I have
seen in his portraits; for in these same books, written
with a moral and religious purpose, such as, for instance, that called "What to do?" in which he has
endeavored to dispense with elegance and suppress
beauty of rhetoric and style, the grace of the artist
flows from his pen in spite of him; his descriptions
are word-paintings, and the hand of the master is
revealed in the admirable conciseness of diction; he
controls every resource of art, and is inspired, will-
he, nill-he. Tolstoï was right in reminding himself
that genius is a divine gift, and there is no law that
can annul it or cast it out.

I cannot believe that Count Tolstoï will persevere in his present path. In the first place, I have little confidence in conversion to a rationalist faith; in the second place, from what I have heard of the disposition of the incomparable novelist, I think it impossible that he should long remain stationary and satisfied. In his vigorous, passionate nature imagination has the strongest part; he is enthusiastic, and given to extremes, like Prince Besukof in "War and Peace;" he is like a fiery charger dashing on at full gallop, that leaps and plunges, and stays not even upon the edge of the precipice. To-day, under the influence of an unbridled sentiment of compassion, he is playing the part of redeemer and apostle; he imitates in his proprietary mansion and in the neighboring towns the primitive fraternal customs of the early Christians; he follows the plough and swings the scythe, and waits on himself, rejecting every offer of service and everything that refines life. To-morrow, perhaps, his lofty understanding will tell him that he was not born to make shoes but novels, and he will perhaps regret having thrown away his best years, the prime of life and creative activity.

At present, he has abandoned himself to the grace of God; and to those of us who are interested in intellectual phenomena, his religious ideas, which are closely interwoven with his imaginative creations, are extremely attractive. "My Religion" contains the fullest exposition of them. He states in it that the whole teaching of Jesus Christ is revealed in one single principle, — that of non-resistance to evil; it is to turn the other cheek, not to judge one's neighbor, not to be angry, not to kill. Tolstoï's experience with the Gospels is like that of the uninitiated who goes into a physical laboratory, and without having any previous instruction wishes to understand at once the management of this or that apparatus or machinery. The sublime and compendious message of the Son of Man has been for nineteen hundred years explained and defined by the loftiest minds in theology and philosophy, who have elucidated every real and profound phase of it as far as is compatible with human needs and laws; but Tolstoï, extracting at pleasure that passage from the sacred Book which most strikes his poetic imagination, deduces therefrom a social state impossible and superhuman; declares tribunals, prisons, authorities, riches, art, war, and armies, iniquitous and reprehensible.

In his earliest years Tolstoï dwelt much on thoughts of the tragedy of war, and in "War and Peace" he gives utterance to some very original and extraordinary, and sometimes even most ingenious opinions concerning it. No historian that I know of can be compared to Tolstoï on this point; none has succeeded in putting in relief the mysterious moral force, the blind and irresistible impulse which determines the great collisions between two peoples independently of the external and trivial causes to which history attributes them. Nor has any one else brought out as clearly as Tolstoï the part played in war by the army, the anonymous mass always sacrificed to the personality of two or three celebrated chiefs, — not only in the campaign bulletins but in the narratives of Clio herself. I believe it will be long before such another man as Tolstoï will arise, not only in the realms of the art of depicting great battle-scenes, but so rich in the gifts of military psychology and physiology; one who can describe the trembling fear in the recruit as well as the strategic calculations of the commander; one who can transfer the impression made upon the soul by the whistling of the bombs carrying death through the air, as well as the sudden impulse that at a certain decisive moment seizes upon thousands of souls that were before vacillating and unstable, lifts them up to a heroic temperature, and decides, in spite of all strategic combinations, the fate of the battle. Though the strenuous enemy of war, Tolstoï is perhaps the man who has written about it better than any other in the world; in every other respect I can compare him to some one else, but not in this. In French writings I recall only one page that could be placed beside Tolstoï's; it is the admirable description of the battle of Waterloo, by Stendhal.

In the name of his own gospel Tolstoï condemns not only human institutions in general, but the Church in particular (the Greek Church, of course), accusing it of having substituted the letter for the spirit, the word of the world for the word of God.

It is not to our purpose to point out Tolstoï's theological errors, but his artistic and social errors fall within the scope of our investigations. We know that, applying the principle of non-resistance in the most rigorous acceptation, he proscribes war, and, as a logical consequence, he disapproves the sacred love of country, which he qualifies as an absurd prejudice, and reproaches himself whenever his own instincts lead him to wish for the triumph of Russia over other nations. In the light of his theory of non-resistance he condemns the revolution, and yet he is forwarding it all the while by his own radical socialism. Tolstoï's social ideal is, not to lift up and instruct the ignorant, nor even to suppress pauperism, but to create a state entirely composed of the poor, to annihilate wealth, luxury, the arts, all delicacy and refinement of custom, and lastly — the lips almost refuse to utter it — even cleanliness and care of the body. Yes, cleanliness and instruction, to wash and to learn, are, in Tolstoï's eyes, great sins, the cause of separation and estrangement among mankind.

Besides this book in which he has set forth his religious ideas, he has written another called "My Confession" and "A Commentary on the Gospels." In "My Confession" he says that having lost faith when very young and given himself up for a time to the vanities of life, and to making literature in which he taught others what he himself knew nothing about, and then turning to science for light upon the enigma of life, he became at last inclined to suicide, when it suddenly occurred to him to look and see how the humbler classes lived, who suffer and toil and know the object of life; and it was borne in upon him that he must follow their example and embrace their simple faith.

Thus Tolstoï formulated the principle enunciated by Gogol, and which is dominant in Russian literature, — the principle of a return to Nature, for which the way was prepared by Schopenhauer, and the sort of modern Buddhism which leads to a subjection of the reason to the animal and the idiot, and a feeling of unbounded tenderness and reverence for inferior creatures.

I have devoted thus much attention to Tolstoï's social and religious ideas, not only because they are interlaced with his novels, and to a certain extent complement and explain them, but because Tolstoï, though he has allied himself with no political party, not even with the Sclavophiles, like Dostoiëwsky, is yet a representative of an order of ideas and sentiments common in his country and proper to it; he is the supreme artist of nihilism and pessimism, and at the same time the apostle of a Christian socialism newly derived from certain theories, dear to the Middle Ages, concerning the eternal Gospels; he is the interpreter, to the world of culture, society, letters, and arts, of that feverish mysticism which manifests itself in more violent forms among certain Russian sects, independent preachers, voluntary mortifiers of the body, the direct inheritors of those who, in dark ages past, declared themselves under the influence of spirits. The spectacle of the socialist fanatic united to the great writer, of the Quietist almost exceeding the limits of evangelical charity joined to the novelist of realism almost *à la* Zola, is so interesting from an intellectual point of view, that it is hard to say which most attracts the attention, Tolstoï or his books.

He has made great mistakes, not the least of which is his renunciation of novel-writing, if indeed that be his intention, though I have heard some Russians affirm the contrary. By condemning the arts and luxuries of urban life, and admitting only the good of the agricultural, for the sake of its simplicity and laboriousness, instead of helping on the Golden Age, he compels a retrogression to the age of the animal, as described by the Roman poet, — "the troglodyte snores, being satisfied with acorns." By anathematizing letters, poetry, theatres, balls, banquets, and all the pleasures of intelligence and civilization, he condemns the most delicate instincts that we possess, sanctions barbarism, justifies a new irruption of Huns and Vandals, and endeavors to arrest the faculty of the perception of the Beautiful, which is a glorious attribute of God himself. And all this for what? To find at the end of this harsh penance not the love of Jesus Christ, who bids us lean on his breast and rest after our labors, but a pantheistic numen, a blind and deaf deity hidden behind a gray mist of abstractions. With sorrow we hear Tolstoï, the great artist, blaspheme when he would pray; hear him spurn the gifts of Heaven, condemn that form of art in which his name shone brightest and shed lustre on his country and all the world, — calling the novel oil poured upon the flames of sensual love, a licentious pastime, food for the senses, and a noxious diversion. We see him, under the hallucination of his mysticism, making shoes and drawing water with the hands that God gave him for weaving forms and designs of artistic beauty into the texture of his marvellous narratives.

V.

FRENCH REALISM AND RUSSIAN REALISM.

THE Russian naturalistic school seems to have reached its culmination in Tolstoï. Concerning Russian naturalism I would say a few words more before leaving the subject. The opinions expressed are impartial, though long confirmed in my own mind.

In recapitulating half a century of Russian literature, we see that this *natural school* followed close upon an imitation of foreign style and an effervescence of romanticism; it was founded by Gogol, and defended by Bielinsky, the estimable critic who did for Russia what Lessing did for Germany. The *natural school* professed the principle of adhering with strict fidelity to the reality, and of copying life exactly in all its humblest and most trivial details. And this new school, born before romanticism was well worn-out, grew and prospered quickly, producing a harvest of novelists even more fertile than the poets of the antecedent school. The date of its appearance was the period denominated *the forties*,—the decade between 1840 and 1850.

The general European political agitation, not being able to manifest itself in Russia by means of insurrections, tumults, and proclamations, took an intellectual form; and young Russia, returning from German universities intoxicated with metaphysics, saturated with liberalism and philanthropy, was eager to pour out its soul, and give vent to its plethora of ideas. A country without lecture-halls, free-press, or political liberty of any sort, had to recur to art as the only refuge. And making use of the sort of subterfuge that love employs when it hides itself under the veil of friendship, the political radical called himself in Russia a sort of left-handed Hegelian, to invent a phrase.

Thus Russian letters, in assuming a national character, showed a strong social and political bias, which contains the clew to its qualities and defects, and especially to its originality. The academic idea of literature as a gentle solace and noble recreation has been for the last half-century less applicable in Russia than anywhere else in the world; never has literature in Russia become a profession as in France, where the writer is prone to become more or less the skilful artisan, quick to observe the variations of public taste, what sort of condiment most tickles its palate, and straightway takes advantage of it, — an artisan satisfied, with honorable exceptions, to sell his wares, and to snap his fingers at the world, at humanity, at France, and even at Paris, exclusive of that strip of asphalt which runs from the Madeleine to the Porte St. Martin. Russian literature stands for more than this; persuaded of the importance of its task, and that it is charged with a great social work and the conduct of the progress of its country, — Holy

Russia, which is itself called to regenerate the world, — neither glory nor gold will satisfy it; its object is to enlighten and to teach the generations. It is but a short step from this to an admonitory and directive literature; and the noblest Russian geniuses have stumbled over this propensity at the end of their literary career. Gogol finished by publishing edificatory epistles, believing them more advantageous than "Dead Souls;" an analogous condition has to-day befallen Tolstoï.

In spite of the severity of Nicholas I., literature enjoyed a relative ease and freedom under his sceptre, either because the Autocrat had a fondness for it, or was not afraid of it. Under the shelter afforded by literature, political Utopias, nihilistic germs, subversive philosophies, and dreams of social regeneration were fostered. The novel — more directly, actively, and efficaciously than the most careful treatises or occasional articles — propagated the seeds of revolution, and being filled with sociological ideas, was devoted to the study of the poor and humble classes, and was marked by realism and sincerity of design; while the flood of indignation consequent upon repressive and violent measures broke forth into copious satire.

In this development of a literature aspiring to transform society, the love of beauty for beauty's sake plays a secondary part, though it is the proper end and aim of all forms of art. Therefore that which receives least attention in the Russian novel is perfection of form, — plot and method best revealing the æsthetic conception. It abounds in superb pages, admirable passages, prodigies of observation, and truth; but, except in the case of Turguenief, the composition is always defective, and there is a sort of incoherence, of palpable and fearful obscurity, amid which we seem to discover gigantic shapes, vaguer but grander than those we are accustomed to see about us.

During a period of twenty or thirty years the novel and the critic were everything to Russia; the national intelligence lived in them, and within their precincts it elaborated a free world after its own heart. Like a maiden perpetually shut away from the outside world, dreaming of some romantic lover whom she has never known or seen, consoling herself with novels, and fancying that all the fine adventures in them have happened to herself, Russia has written into the national novel her own visionary nature, her thirst for political adventures, and her eagerness for transcendental reforms. One most important reform may be said to be directly the work of the novel, namely, the emancipation of the serfs.

When the more clement Alexander II. succeeded the austere Nicholas I., and the restraints laid upon the political press were loosened so that it could spread its wings, the novel suffered in consequence. The hope of great events to come, the approaching liberation of the serfs, the formation of a sort of liberal cabinet, the efflorescence of new illusions that bud under every new régime, concurred to infuse the literature with civic and social tendencies. Beautiful and bright and poetical is art for art's sake, and as Puchkine understood it; but at the hour of doubt and strife we ask even art for positive service and practical solutions. Who stops to see whether the life-preservers thrown to drowning men struggling with death are of elegant workmanship?

In speaking of nihilism I have mentioned the most important one of the directive Russian novels, called "What to Do?" by the martyr Tchernichewsky, — a work of no great literary merit, but which was the gospel of young Russia. In his wake followed a host of novelists of this tendency, but inferior, obscure, and without even the inventive power of their leader in dressing up their ideas as symbolic personages, like his ascetic socialist Rakmetof, who laid himself down upon a board stuck through with nail-points. In their turn came the reactionaries, or rather the conservatives, and in novels as absurd as those of their predecessors they clothed the nihilists in purple and gold; it finally resulted that everybody was as ready to produce a novel as to write a serious article, or to handle a gun at a barricade. If any one of the neophytes of the school of directive novels possessed genius, it was swallowed up in the froth of political passion.

As an accomplice in guilt, criticism did not weigh these works of art in the golden scales of Beauty, but in the leaden ones of Utility. There were critics who went so far as to declare war upon art, undertaking to ruin the fame of great authors, because they wrought not in the interests of transcendentalism; their motive was like that which impelled the early Christians to destroy the great works of paganism.

The popular novelists condemned the verses of Puchkine and the music of Glinka, in the name of the down-trodden and suffering people, just as Tolstoï, in remembrance of the hungry family he had just visited, refused to partake of the appetizing meal offered him by servants in livery. As art had not achieved the amelioration of the people's condition, they considered it not merely a futile recreation, but actually an obnoxious thing. Bielinsky, with a taint of this same mania, at last entertained scruples against the pure pleasure enjoyed in contemplation of the beautiful, and was almost inclined to stop his ears and shut his eyes so as not to fall into æsthetic sins.

Are the authors and critics the only ones responsible for this directive character of most Russian novels? No. Two factors are requisite to the work of art, — the artist and the public. The Russians exact more of the novel than we; the Latins, at least, regard the novel as a means of beguiling a few evening hours, or a summer siesta, — a way to kill time. Not so the Russians. They demand that the novelist shall be a prophet, a seer of a better future, a guide of new generations, a liberator of the serf, able to face tyranny, to redeem the country, to reveal the ideal, in fine, an evangelist and an apostle. Given this conception, it ought not to astonish us that the students drag Turguenief's carriage through the streets, that they faint with emotion at Dostoiëwsky's touch, nor that the enthusiasm of the multitude — in itself contagious — should sometimes fill the heads of the novelists themselves. The novelists are, in reality and truth, a faithful echo of the aspirations and needs of the souls that feed upon their works. The Occidentalism of Turguenief, the mysticism of Dostoiëwsky, the pessimism of Tolstoï, the charity, the revolutionary spirit, — each is a manifestation of the national atmosphere condensed in the brains of two or three foremost geniuses. Who can doubt the reflex action which the anonymous multitude exercises on eminent persons, when he contemplates the great Russian novelists?

There is a difference, however, between the novel which is purposely directive, the novel with a moral, so to speak, and the novel which is guided by a social drift, by "the spirit of the times." The former is liable to mediocrity and flatness, the latter is the patrimony of the loftiest minds. This spirit, this social sympathy, issued from every pore of Ivan Turguenief, the most able and exquisite of them all, indirectly and without detriment to his impersonality, and with the full conviction that it ought to be so; and novel-writing is useful in this way and no other. He says as much in a sort of autobiographical fragment, in which he explains how and why he left his country: "I felt that I must at all costs get away from my enemy in order the better to deal him a telling blow. And my enemy bore a well-known name; it was serfdom, slavery. Under the name of slavery I included everything that I proposed to fight without truce and to the death. This was my oath, and I was not alone in subscribing thereto. And in order to be faithful to it I came to the Occident."

If I am not mistaken, the great difference between French and Russian naturalism lies in this predominant characteristic of social expression. The defects and merits of French naturalism are bound up with its condition as a purely literary insurrection and protest against the rhetoric of romanticism. In vain Zola exerts his Titanic energies to impress on his works this social significance, whose invigorating power is not unheeded by his perspicacious mind. He fights against egoism without and perhaps within; but only in the two which he conceives to be his master works, " L'Assommoir " and " Germinal," has he approached the desired mark.

The condition of France is diametrically opposed to that of Russia. I am only repeating the opinion of a large number of illustrious Frenchmen who have judged themselves without any great amount of optimism. They say, "We are an old people, depraved and worn-out, our illusions vanished, our hopes faded. We have proved all things, and now we cannot be moved either by military glory which has undone and ruined us, or by revolutions which have discredited us and made Europe look upon us with suspicion. We have no religious faith, nor even social faith. We desire peace, and, if possible, that industry and commerce may flourish; we are not yet bereft of patriotism, and we expect art to entertain us, which is difficult, — for what new thing remains for the artist to discover? Criticism, spread abroad among the multitudes, has killed inspiration; the generative forces are exhausted. We demand so much of the novelists that they are at a loss how to whet our appetites, and neither ugliness, nor unnatural crime, nor monstrous aberrations are sufficient to stimulate our cloyed palates. They are touched with our coldness, and, like ourselves, spiritless and inert, sick and disgusted, they feel beforehand the irremediable and fatal decadence that is coming upon us, and they believe that art in the Latin races will die with the century." Thus mourn some of the men of France, and to my mind they have a basis of truth.

The artist never goes beyond the line marked out by his epoch. And how should he? Of course there is, in every work of art, something that is the exclusive property of the individual, something of his own genius; but as the nature of the fish is to swim, but swim it cannot out of the water, and the nature of the bird is to fly, but lacking air it flies not, so, given a social atmosphere, the artist modifies and adapts himself to it. The novelist cannot have an ideal different from the society which reads him; and if one but perceives the rigor and inflexibility of this law, one may avoid many foolish sentiments expressed with the intent to censure the immorality of the novel. Take any one of them, Tolstoï's, Zola's, Goncourt's, Dostoiëwsky's, look at it well, study it closely, and you will find in it the exact expression and even the artistic interpretation of a tendency of his epoch, his nation, and his race. This is as evident as that two and two make four. Novelists are what they must be rather than what they would be, and it is not in their power to make a world after their own hearts or according to any ideal pattern.

Melchior de Voguié, it seems to me, has not recognized this truth in accusing French novelists of materialism, dryness, egoism, and paganism, and has not taken into account the fact that the reflex action of the public upon the novelist is greater than that of the latter upon the former, or at least that the novelist is the first to be influenced, although afterward his works have an influence in turn, and in lesser proportion.

"The French realists," says Voguié, "ignore the better part of humanity, which is the spirit." This is true; and I have said and thought for a long time that realism, to realize to the full its own program, must embrace matter and spirit, earth and heaven, human and superhuman. I entirely agree with Voguié in believing that naturalism — or to call it by a more comprehensive name, the School of Truth or Realism — should not close its eyes to the mystery that is beyond rational explanations, nor deny the divine as a known quantity. And so entirely is this my opinion, that I could never consent to the narrow and short-sighted idea of some who imagine that a Catholic, by the act of admitting the supernatural, the miraculous, and the verity of revelation, is incapacitated for writing a profound, serious, and good novel, a realistic novel, a novel that shall breathe a fragrant essence of truth. Aside from the fact that literary as well as scientific methods do not presuppose a negation of religion, when did it ever happen that Catholicism, in the days of liveliest faith, impeded the production of the best of realist novels, as for example " Don Quixote "? The truth is that the novel, given the epic element, will be neither Catholic nor religious in those societies which are neither one nor the other. The lyric element does not demand this harmony with society: a great Catholic poet may be found in a most agnostic country, but not a Catholic novelist.

The novel is a clear mirror, a faithful expression of society, and the actual conditions of the novel in Europe are a proof of it. I think I have shown that the Russian novel reflects the dreams, sentiments, and changes of that country; it appears revolutionary and subversive, because the spirit of both Russian *intelligence* and Russian educated people is so. In France, where to-day, in spite of the efforts of the spiritual and eclectic school, the traditions of the Encyclopædia have prevailed together with a frivolous sensualist materialism, the novel follows this road also, and without meaning to strike up Béranger's famous refrain, —

> " C'est la faute de Rousseau,
> C'est la faute de Voltaire,"

I affirm that *animalism*, determined materialism, pessimism, and *decadentism* may be explained by the light of the great writers of the eighteenth century, not only through their literary influence, but because the society which pores over the novels of the present day is the daughter of the French Revolution, and the latter is the daughter of the Encyclopædia. Who does not know the relation which exists between the novel and the fashion in England, and how the former is conditioned, shaped, and limited exclusively by the latter? In Germany another curious phenomenon is apparent. The novel in vogue is historical, — a condition appropriate to a country where everybody is interested only in epic life and the contingency of war.

On account of this interdependence, or, in fact, unity, of the novel and society, I cannot agree with Voguié when he says that the books that are influencing and stimulating the multitudes, the general ideas that are transforming Europe, are proceeding nowadays not from France but from Russia. It may be true of the Northern races, but of Latin races it cannot be more than partially and indirectly so. Does Voguié find in the French novel as in the Russian the latent fermentation of the evangelical spirit, or are the currents of mysticism that impregnate Russia circulating through France?

Russia is Christian, in spite of German materialist philosophers who for a time set her brains in a whirl, but whom she has finally rejected, as the sea gives up a dead body; and if I have succeeded in showing clearly the forms adopted by the social revolution in Russia, and the strange analogies these sometimes bear to the actions of the early Christians, if I have shown the love of sacrifice, the ardent charity, the sympathetic pity and tenderness not only toward the oppressed but toward even the criminal, the despised, the idiot, and the outcast, which characterize this society and this literature; if I have shown the degrees of mystic fervor by which it is permeated and consumed, — no one need be surprised at my statement and conclusion that although Buddha and Schopenhauer have a goodly share in the present condition of Russian thought, the larger part is nevertheless Christian. It is my opinion that the world is more Christian now than in the Middle Ages, not as to faith, but as to sentiments and customs; and if in hours of despondency I were sometimes inclined to doubt the efficiency of the word of Christ, the sight of its prodigious effects in Russia would certainly correct my doubts. The heterodox nature of the Russian faith is not a nullification of it. The most heretical heretic, if he be a sincere Christian, has more of truth than error in his faith. But error is like sin: one drop of poison is enough to permeate a glass of pure water; yet it is certain that there is more water than poison in the glass.

To return to the literary question, the Russian novel demonstrates, if such demonstration be necessary, the futility of the censures directed against naturalism, and which confound general principles with the circumstances and social conditions which environ the novelist. The Russian novel proves that all the precepts of the art of naturalism may be realized and fulfilled without committing any of those sins of which it is accused by those who know it through the medium of half a dozen French novels. The charge that is oftenest made against the French realist is the having painted pictures of passion and vice too nakedly and with too much candor, — and the charge is certainly not without foundation; and it may be added that some novelists overload the canvas and go to the extreme of making humanity out to be more sinful than even physical possibilities admit; but they must not be made to bear the responsibility alone; the public that gloats and feeds on these comfits, and grumbles when they are not provided, — the public, I say, must share it. In Russia, where the readers do not ask the novelist for intricate plot or high-colored sketches, the novel is chaste: I do not mean in the English sense of being moral with an air of affectation, and frowns and false modesty; I mean chaste without effort, like an ancient marble statue. In "Anna Karénina" Tolstoï depicts an illicit passion, extravagant, vehement, full of youthful ardor; yet there is not a page of "Anna Karénina" which cannot be read aloud and without a blush. In "War and Peace" the most candid pages are models of decorum, of true decorum, such as education, reason, and the dignity of man approve. In " Crime and Punishment" Dostoiëwsky introduces the character of a prostitute; but this character is no such romantic creature as Marie Gautier or Nana. She is not made poetical, nor is she embellished or exaggerated; yet she produces an impression (let him read the novel who doubts) of purity, of suffering, of austerity. In Turguenief, by far the most sensual of the great Russian novelists, and in Pisemsky, of secondary rank, there is so much art in the disposition and harmony of detail and description, that the definitive impression, while less severe than in the case of the two others mentioned, is equally noble and lofty.

Are they any the less Realists for this? They are rather more so, in my opinion. In order to carry out the great precept of modern art, the novelist must copy life,—the life that we live and that unfolds about us every day. But life does not unfold as it is represented in many novels that are the product of French naturalism. The Zola school makes use of abstraction and accumulation in uniting in one scene and one character all the aberrations, abominations, and vices that only a collection of profligates could be capable of, with the result offered us in pictures such as the house in "Pot-Bouille," that should be handled with tongs for fear of soiling one's fingers. We turn to the reality, and we find that all these colors exist, that all these vices are actual,—yes, but one at a time, intermingled with a thousand good or commonplace things; then we are in a rage with the novelist, and ever after bear him a grudge for having a mania for ugliness. The impression which life makes upon us is quite different; the alternative of good is evil, of poetry is vulgarity; we demand a recognition of this from the novelist, and this the Russian novelists have given us, yet without leaving the firm ground of realist art. They present the material, the bestial, the trivial, the vile, the obscene, the passionate, as they appear in life, in due proportion and no more.

We have also to thank them for having recognized the psychical life, and the spiritual, moral, and religious needs of mankind. And I would make a distinction between the moral spirit of the English novel and the Russian. The English judge of human actions according to preconceived notions derived from a general standard accepted by society and officially imposed by custom and the Protestant religion. The Russian moralist feels deeper and thinks higher; morality is not for him a system of narrow and inalterable rules, but the aspiration of a creature advancing toward a higher plane, and learning his lessons in the hard school of truth and the great theatre of art.

The spiritual element in the Russian novel is to me one of its most singular merits. The novel should not teach the supernatural, nor be the instrument of any religious propaganda. But from this premise to a condition of mutilation and mere dry chronicle of physiological functions is a long way. There are countless facts of our existence that cannot be explained by the most determined materialist; it is not the duty of art to explain them, but art cannot justly ignore them. Émile Zola is both a thinker and an artist. As an artist he is admirable, and is hardly behind Tolstoï either in poetic or descriptive faculties; but with the artist he combines the philosopher — may I call it so? — the philosopher of the lowest and coarsest fibre, whose influence upon French naturalism has been most pernicious, and has greatly limited the scope of the novel in his country.

In conclusion, it is my opinion that the only way to understand the naturalistic movement is in connection with its social environment; the impulse of our age toward a representation of truth in art everywhere prevails, and everywhere the novel has become a result of observation, an analytical study, as we notice in a general view of European literature for the last forty years. The century which began with lyric poetry is closing with a triumphant novel.

But the great principle of reality is differently applied in different countries. Why was romanticism so much the same in England, Germany, Spain, and Russia? Because it was chiefly rhetoric, — a literary protest, an artistic insurrection. And why the differences between French naturalism, the Russian *natural school*, English and Spanish realism, and Italian *verismo?* Because each one of these phases of the religion of truth is adequate to the country that conceived it, and to the hour and the occasion upon which it is focused. It is no objection that between these various forms there is close communication and relation. Edmund de Goncourt once remarked to me that the Russian novel is not so original as people think, for besides the marked influence of Hoffmann and Edgar Poe upon the genius of Dostoiëwsky, it would not be difficult to trace in the other great writers the inspiration of Balzac, Flaubert, Stendhal, and George Sand. He was right; and yet Russian literature is not the less indigenous.

I should always prefer the art that is disinterested, that carries within itself its aim and object, to the art that is directive, with a moral purpose; between the art that is pagan and the art that is imbecile, I should choose the pagan. If we Spaniards, who are like the Russians, at once an ancient and a young people, still ignorant of what the future may lead us to, and never able to make our traditions harmonize with our aspirations, — if we could succeed in incorporating in our novel not merely bits of fragmentary reality, artistic individualisms, but the spirit, the heart, the blood of our country, what we are doing, what we are feeling as a whole, — it would indeed be well. Yet I think this impossible, not for lack of talent but for lack of preparation on the part of the public, upon whom at present the novel exercises no influence at all. The novel is read neither quantitatively nor qualitatively in Spain. As to quantity, let the authors who publish, and the booksellers who sell, speak what they know; of the quality, let the numerous lovers of Montepin and the eager readers of the translations in the *feuilletines* tell us. The serious and profound novel dies here without an echo; criticism makes no comment upon it, and the public ignores its appearance. Is there a single modern novel that is popular, in the true meaning of the word, among us? Has any novel had any influence at all in Spanish political, social, or moral life?

On coming from France, I have often noticed a significant fact, which is, that at the French station of Hendaye there is a stand for the sale of all the popular and celebrated novels; while at Irun, just across the frontier, only a few steps away, but Spanish, there is nothing to be had but a few miserable, trashy books, and not a sign of even our own best novelists' works. From the moment we set foot on Spanish soil the novel, as a social element, disappears. It is sad to say, but it is so true that it would be madness to build any illusions on this matter. And yet the instinct, the desire, the inexplicable anxiety of the artist to embody and transmit the great truths of life, the impulse that lifts men to great deeds, and to desire to be the voice of the people, is secretly stimulating the Spanish novelists to break the ice of general indifference, to put themselves in communication with the sixty million souls and intelligences that to-day speak our language. Is the goal which we desire to attain inaccessible? Perhaps; but as the immense difficulties in the way of penetrating to the Arctic regions and the discovery of the open Polar Sea are but an incentive to the explorer, so the impossible in this undertaking should incite and spur on the masters of the Iberian novel.

A few words of humble confession, and I have done.

I feel that there is a certain indecision and ambiguity running through these essays of mine. I could not quite condemn the revolution in Russia, nor could I altogether approve its doctrines and discoveries. A book must reflect an intellectual condition which, in my case, is one of uncertainty, vacillation, anxiety, surprise, and interest. My vision has not been perfectly clear, therefore I have offered no conclusive judgments,—for conviction and affirmation can only proceed from the mind they have mastered. Russia is an enigma; let those solve it who can,—I could not. The Sphinx called to me; I looked into the depths of her eyes, I felt the sweet and bewildering attraction of the unknown, I questioned her, and like the German poet I wait, with but moderate hope, for the answer to come to me, borne by voices of the ocean of Time.

THE END.

www.ingramcontent.com/pod-product-compliance
Lightning Source LLC
Chambersburg PA
CBHW032053230426
43672CB00009B/1574